Mirror Images

Seeing ourselves in other people

DAVID ADAM

Illustrations by
Monica Capoferri

First published in Great Britain in 2007

Society for Promoting Christian Knowledge
36 Causton Street
London SW1P 4ST

British Library Cataloguing-in-Publication Data
A catalogue record for this book is available from the British Library

ISBN-13: 978–0–281–05774–0
ISBN-10: 0–281–05774–5

1 3 5 7 9 10 8 6 4 2

Typeset in 11/13.5pt Minion by Graphicraft Ltd, Hong Kong
Printed in Great Britain by Bookmarque Ltd, Croydon, Surrey

Contents

Place your mind before the mirror of eternity!
Place your soul in the brilliance of glory!
Place your heart in the figure of the divine substance!
And transform your whole being into the image of the
Godhead itself through contemplation.

(Clare of Assisi, *c.* 1193–1253)

Introduction

At home when the discussion got around to a person and their fashions or their attitudes to life, it was amazing how many different points of view we could come up with. If we were getting too critical or judgemental my mother would say, 'Have you looked in the mirror lately?' The implication of this was always the same, 'If you want to make such judgements look at yourself.'

Now with some trepidation, I want to present to you a small number of people that I have encountered in nearly 50 years of pastoral ministry. These people have caused me to reflect on my own life and my faith. By them I have been enriched, brought to tears, had a glimpse of glory, and often changed my own direction. I bring them before you as mirrors of our own strengths and weaknesses: mirrors in which we recognize familiar reactions and expressions; mirrors that confront us with mystery and awe. All are like a glimpse in a mirror, moments that were fleeting and cannot be held. All are more wonderful than the reflections I bring before you, more solid and more liable to change.

In *Mirror Images* I want to look at people and how they reflect certain attitudes we have to life: how various individuals show characteristics that we all have a tendency to have. In our meeting with other people we often see images of our own reactions and attitudes. Sometimes this is a clear image and it helps us to see ourselves more clearly. Sometimes it is a distorted image that reaches down into our deepest fears. Then at other times we see a bright image that gives us for a moment a glimpse of the glory that is ours.

At all times we need to respect the person who comes before us. People cannot be given a label or a number: we should not call them names that suggest that is the only way to view them, such as 'hysteric', 'religious', 'atheist' or 'fool'. They are not fixed images like a photograph or a painting: they are living, moving and changing beings. We never see the whole picture and we can come away with a false image of that person. The people that come before us are not for our entertainment or even for our scrutiny but for our attention and our reflection. We must remember that whatever we look at we alter at least in some small way. Those who have had to do their work under the eyes of an inspector know how true this is. In meeting with anyone, we should respect the mystery and wonder they present to us. Every person has many facets and some facets are better than others. No one is reducible to one aspect of his or her life. The 'Bird Man' that you will meet is also a family man, a husband and father. He is also an active member of the community in which he lives. He works for the Fire Service and often helps in rescue work. Yet we only look at his attitude to birds for it shows a deep respect for creation and for life that we all need.

Whenever we are treated as an object for scrutiny or counted as a statistic we have a right to feel uncomfortable for that is only a small part of us. I can remember being deeply moved by Alan Sillitoe's *The Loneliness of the Long Distance Runner*. I had not long been ordained but was already being treated more as a 'Reverend' than a human being. I even seemed to lose my name, to be called 'Vicar' or 'Curate'. It usually guaranteed me a seat by myself on a bus or a train. In Sillitoe's book the runner is a Borstal boy who is to compete against a local public school. The governor of the Borstal is keen for the boy to win. The boy is aware that it is not out of respect for him or concern for him as a person. He needs to win for the glory of the governor and the Borstal. The governor thinks no more of the boy than he would of a racehorse he has never seen but upon which he has placed a bet. In bitterness the boy says,

> And I'll lose that race, because I am not a race horse at all, and I'll let him know about it when I am about to get out ... I'm a human being and I've thoughts and secrets and bloody life inside me that he doesn't know is there, and he'll never know that because he is stupid.
>
> (Sillitoe, 1960)

In the same way Shylock in *The Merchant of Venice* complains at being treated as a 'Jew' but not as a human,

> I am a Jew. Hath not a Jew eyes? hath not a Jew hands, organs, dimensions, senses, affections, passions? fed with the same food, hurt with the same weapons, subject to the same diseases, healed by the same means, warmed and cooled by the same winter and summer, as a Christian is? If you prick us, do we not bleed? if you tickle us, do we not laugh? if you poison us, do we not die? and if you wrong us, shall we not revenge? If we are like you in the rest, we will resemble you in that.
>
> (*The Merchant of Venice*, Act 3 scene 1)

We must always respect the fact that any person that we encounter has thoughts and secrets and life beyond our knowing. In meeting with anyone, we are confronted with a deep mystery and an 'otherness'.

In meeting with any other person, there is always the opportunity to meet the Great Other who is God. I believe that if we are insensitive to other people we will not be sensitive to God. If we are bad at listening to others we are not likely to heed the Word of God. We need to be open to people as they are and not what we think they should be: we need to approach people with eyes cleansed and with an open mind. Too often we impose upon people our own jaundiced views. It is when we are attentive and open to the other, be it person or thing, that the mystery of the Great Other can then approach us. Through the mystery of life and of creation we come with awe before the mystery of God.

Folk tales often reflect how life is; within them there is always a battle between good and evil. We learn how love transforms the beast and how the frog prince is liberated. Such tales often illustrate the corrupting power of sin and at the same time the hope of redemption. We learn that the broken can be restored and that hearts can be renewed. Folk tales are popular because they mirror for us the human condition. One of my favourite tales is 'The Snow Queen'.

The magic mirror in 'The Snow Queen' by Hans Christian Andersen is very frightening for it shows how distorted our views of life can become. We are told of the mirror 'that everything good and beautiful when reflected in it, shrank up to almost nothing, whilst things which were ugly and useless were magnified and made to appear ten times worse than before'. Now I know some people who are just like that; reporting of world events on the news is often like that. I wonder how much I am like that. The story continues: 'The loveliest landscapes reflected in this mirror looked like boiled spinach; and the handsomest persons appeared ugly, or as if standing on their heads; their features so distorted that their friends could never have recognized them.' I hope in presenting this narrow view of multifaceted individuals I do not do them an injustice. Throughout *Mirror Images* I have changed names of individuals and the places where I have met them. In the main I have shown a single facet only of a person to help us see ourselves a little more clearly. I will look at a bird-lover who is full of reverence and respect for the world about him, the partially blind man who could see God's glory more clearly than many with full sight, the control freak who can only allow things to happen the way he wants. Then there is a beautiful young woman who discovers that 'love changes everything': she is my Snow White figure who is wasting away from lack of love. I look at the one who is possessed by sport and hyperactivity yet has a deep emptiness. In all these people I see myself at some stage of my life. Not one person comes to be criticized; only to reflect for us our own reactions to life.

There is a 'reality show' on television – how contrived are all these shows – that puts its contestants into a room with mirrors on every wall. Then the person is asked to look at herself and say what she sees. An all-round look is very different from a single mirror. Added to this they usually have to remove some of their clothing and face the comments of two people. It takes a lot of courage to do this but the end result is usually transforming for a while at least. I hope I have gained a better all-round view from the people I have met and from the suggestions they have made to my own way of living.

When the making of mirrors became easier, King Christian IV of Denmark in the mid-seventeenth century built the Rosenborg Palace in a park not far from the centre of Copenhagen. He included in this grand house a small room that had mirrored walls, floor and ceiling. In this room one might stand on a mirrored floor and see one's reflection above and on all sides. An image that appeared not only once but seemed to continue into infinity. I am not sure whether this was a pursuit of truth or just vanity but it must have been very sobering for many who entered this room.

The story of the Snow Queen's mirror is often in my thoughts. It was declared that: 'by its means the world and its inhabitants might be seen for the first time as they really are'. The story tells us that this mirror fell to earth, breaking into millions, billions and trillions of pieces with fragments smaller than a grain of sand getting into people's eyes and causing them to see everything in a wrong way or to have eyes only for what is perverted or corrupt. Some splinters entered the hearts of people and that was terrible. The heart became cold and hard like a lump of ice. Again I have met people so troubled, with a jaundiced view of all of life, and others who have allowed their hearts to become cold. We are told that there are still splinters of this mischievous mirror flying about in the air. I don't doubt it!

Another great story is 'Snow White' by the Brothers Grimm in which there is a wonderful mirror that can speak. The wicked queen could see herself in it and be told of her beauty. But the mirror was honest and by the time Snow White was seven she was more beautiful than anyone. When the queen asked,

> Mirror, mirror on the wall,
> Who is the fairest one of all?

The mirror replied:

> Thou, queen may'st fair and beauteous be,
> But Snow White is lovelier far than thee.

The wicked queen could not stand the truth and set about to destroy Snow White. One of the reasons for the crucifixion of Jesus was that people could not bear to face the truth about themselves. If you fear honesty about yourself or if you are unwilling to look in the mirror, this is not the book for you.

Stop here before you are confronted with people who might show you what you are like. The wicked queen shows how poisonous jealousy and self-centredness really are and at the same time the story of Snow White shows us the redeeming characters of some people who could be described as strange.

After looking at people I have met, I will then present to you certain biblical characters and look at them in the same way. A child once persistently interrupted me as I told a story; he kept asking 'Am I in that story?' We spent a good deal of time discussing whether he was a 'goodie' or a 'baddie' and where he wanted to be in the story. I am sure I learnt far more than he did as we reflected on each character. Jesus told his parables because they reflected our situation in the world, so in them we can see an image of ourselves. In the same way biblical characters reveal the same human traits and needs as we have so we can see in them a reflection of our own way of living.

For example, 2 Samuel illustrates this well in Nathan's encounter with David. You might like to read 2 Samuel 11.1— 12.7. David is seen as a good king, he 'reigned over all Israel; and David administered justice and equity to all his people' (2 Samuel 8.15). David is one of the great heroes of the Old Testament. Suddenly we are confronted with another side of the man. David took a wrong turning and a big one at that. The Bible could have omitted this event but David is shown with 'warts and all'. Yet in doing so it shows how this ancestor of Jesus was human after all. He has emotions and failures like all of us and yet God still works through him. Though David had other wives, he lusted after another man's wife whom he saw bathing. David sent messengers to bring her to the king's house and there he committed adultery with her. Bathsheba became pregnant. David brought Uriah her husband back from the battlefield. He tried to persuade Uriah to sleep with his wife so that he would believe that when the baby was born it was his. When this did not work he sent Uriah to the front line of the fighting and told Joab to put Uriah where the fighting was the fiercest and then draw back from him. The enemy killed Uriah, though it was David that as good as murdered him. It is sad to see how often power corrupts people. Now David was free to make Bathsheba his wife.

Nathan the prophet of God somehow heard of all that had happened. Whether it was common knowledge whispered in the court we do not know but Nathan knew and could not keep silent. Nathan tells David a story about two men: one rich, one poor. The rich man had many flocks and herds; the poor man had nothing but one little ewe lamb that grew up with his family and that was kept like a pet. When the rich man had a visitor he was loath to take one of his sheep to feed the man so he took the poor man's ewe lamb. David was very angry when he heard of this injustice and said, 'As the Lord lives, this man deserves to die.' Without flinching, Nathan said to David, 'You are the man.' A brave prophet, and a king who saw mirrored in another what he had at that moment become. Like David, often the people I do not like are those who show my own weakness and failures.

In our looking at others it is well worth considering what sort of image we present to them. We need learn from those who show us what we could be like or what we should not be like. In my looking at others and seeing an image of my hopes and fears I often pray the words of Robbie Burns:

> O wad some Pow'r the giftie gie us
> To see oursels as others see us!
> It wad frae mony a blunder free us,
> An' foolish notion.
>
> ('To a Louse', Robert Burns, 1786)

A last theme that should be present in our thoughts is that we are all made in the image of God. We are God's icon and so should reflect something of his grace, goodness and glory. True the 'image of God' is often hidden but it is not lost. The image may be covered over by much dust, dirt and debris but it is still there. The image may even be defaced but it has not been effaced. Often 'God's image' in us has been covered over by years of neglect. But we are given the chance again and again to be the mirror image of God. In the same way, if we look carefully, we can find the image of God in those that we meet. This may not often be stated in this book but it is there as an underlying theme.

The Earth is the Lord's

I had two hard days in a row. On the Friday I went to the cremation of a friend whom I had known for a long time. He was a wonderful character and had been so full of life. Over the last few years he had done quite a lot of noteworthy things within his local community. He was a multi-talented person and greatly loved by many. The service was impersonal, with hardly a mention of his name, never mind his life. The minister had in no way tried to find out anything about him. We were presented with platitudes. The music was the kind you get in a supermarket and there were no hymns. 'Death' seemed to be a word to be avoided. This meant that the hope of resurrection could hardly come into the event. The blandness and hollowness of the service was painful. At a precious time, when lives are waiting for some guidance, comfort and hope, we were offered nothing. I felt that if this is what the Church offers no wonder so many are not attracted. I found the service depressing and was sorry for so many friends that had come truly to celebrate a life and to mourn a friend's departure. I was feeling a little raw but the hollowness of the whole affair hurt.

On the Saturday I went to a wedding in the local Register Office. I did not object to the place in any way as the couple were not churchgoers. I wanted to celebrate with them the joy of their love. The registrar's was up two flights of stairs that were dingy and uncarpeted. The paper must have been on the walls for years. The room was filled with a clutter of books and there was just room for the 18 of us. There was nowhere for anyone to sit. The person who took the ceremony seemed to be in a hurry to get it over. Maybe there was another due in a few minutes. There was no chance to relish the words or the occasion. In fact, she seemed to treat the words almost as a joke. There was no moment that affirmed the seriousness of the vows or the joy of the couple's love. Perhaps at the back of my mind I feared that I have known church weddings not far removed from this. I have known cold, uncared-for churches where those who come receive little more respect than was given to the building. I was worried that this is the way life seems to be going for so many and how little guidance many of our young couples are given. I was determined to keep an eye on how I conducted worship and how I dealt with the important moments in the lives of people. I wanted to be as sure as possible the celebration of Communion that I shared in on Sunday was a celebration. I wanted the service I did to affirm life and love as well as the presence and power of God.

After the Sunday Communion, Neville approached me, 'There were some special moments in the service today. I especially liked the silences at the peak times.' I was delighted on two scores, for Neville rarely came to church when he came to the island; he usually sent the rest of his family and at least something had touched him (more than my words!). Neville continued, 'How about coming with me tomorrow morning to hear the dawn chorus and see what we might see? We can be back in time for you to do your morning service. We will set off at 4.30 a.m.' Before I had time to think I had agreed. Blimey! Out by 4.30 a.m.! Some folk are dedicated.

As his hobby Neville was a bird-photographer, though he was just as happy to watch them and hear them. He had been known to stay in a bird hide all night just to be there at the right time. Yet he was not fanatical about it and was quite humble in the way he related what he had heard and seen. He said he was a bird-photographer for the sheer joy of capturing fleeting moments or even just for the thrill of being there. His comment on one such encounter was,

> I once saw a phalarope at Newton-by-the-Sea. It was so tame I could almost have touched it. It still was in full colour and its red throat glowed. I might never see the like again but I was there, I saw it and I will remember it for ever.

This sensitivity was in direct contrast to another man I knew who was a photographer of birds; note how the photography takes the prime place. This man would doctor a nest so that he could get a better shot. He cut twigs away from around a nest for a better view. This would leave the eggs visible to predators but he got his photographs. I fell out with this man when he moved a barn owl's nest so that he could get a better shot of the young. The next day the young had disappeared and the barn owl that had nested there for a good few years did not return. Neville was not like that for he had a great respect for the birds and said each one should be treated with 'reverence'. He also said at one time, 'We should remember that the earth is the Lord's and all that is in it. God is not to be found only in church or in the study of books.'

Neville arrived on the dot. I was aware that if you want to see anything special or do anything out of the ordinary you have to be willing to exert yourself, to put yourself out. One of the greatest efforts at all times is to make sure you are there. Too often we come to the present distracted and we do not give full attention to the people we are with. Birdwatching is a great way of learning how to be still and quiet yet attentive and alert. It is a waiting with all the senses tuned to what is around you. There is little difference between this stillness and waiting in quiet before God.

We were fortunate that it was a beautiful May morning. Today's trip was not physically extending. It was only a 30-minute ride and then a five-minute walk. How easy it is to step out of our familiar world and its routine and into something new and different. As we stepped out of the car we heard the bubbling cascade of the curlew calling over the moorland and a lapwing with its pee-ee-wit as it rose from its nesting place. Then, for me a magic moment, the cuckoo called. This was the first time I had heard it that year. Neville drew my attention to the up-and-down song of a goldcrest. I never would have heard it without his help. In the same way he drew my attention to the gargling warble of the blackcap – heard but not seen. Neville continued to identify birds by their sounds. I had to trust his knowledge and sometimes his hearing for sometimes I failed not only to discern the sound but also to hear it. Already the day was like experiencing the dawn of creation with light and life and beauty all around us.

Neville led me to a leafy hideaway near a waterfall. 'This is one of the things I wanted you to see,' he said in awed tones. 'It is a dipper's nest.' I know even if I had gone there alone I would have walked past the nest without seeing it. The blackish-brown bird with white throat and breast was tucked into the edge of the waterfall. It was a wonderful image of peace. The water was hurtling down quite close to it but it was in no way disturbed. It left its nest briefly and then returned. We watched it for about half an hour. The silence was only broken by birdsong and the sound of the water. There was a feeling of belonging to a wonderful world. On this occasion Neville did not use his camera. He just repeated more than once, 'It's a joy to be here; a joy to be alive.'

On the short journey back Neville reminded me of the story I had told him about St Kevin, and its deeper meaning. The story could have come only from Ireland or from the Desert Fathers!

Kevin lived in the beautiful area of Glendalough in Ireland in the late sixth to seventh century. Kevin used to often pray with his arms outstretched, possibly making the shape of a cross. Many of the Celtic saints liked to pray in 'cross vigil' as it was called. While Kevin was praying a blackbird came and began to build a nest on Kevin's outstretched hand. Kevin did not move. He let the bird take her time and build the nest. When the nest was completed the blackbird laid her eggs. So Kevin kept as still as possible so as not to disturb the bird as she sat. Kevin waited there in stillness until the birds hatched, fledged and finally flew away. Then Kevin was able to lower his arms and continue with other work. Now that really is an Irish story. No human could have stayed like that for the weeks that were involved. Yet the story is full of meaning. It wants us to reflect what is implied within it. Everyone who prays is linked to God through Christ and the cross. Prayer itself is not a leisurely occupation; it is often costly if not even painful at times. Anyone who prays to the Creator must have a reverence and respect for his creation. If our relationship with the world is wrong then our relationship to its Creator cannot be comfortable. How can we say we love God if we destroy or misuse his creation? In being one with God in prayer, Kevin was also at one with God's world.

Neville remembered this almost better than I did. He quietly talked about the troubles of our planet due to our misuse of its resources. He pointed out that the demise of so many birds in our part of the world was due to the changes in our patterns of farming. The shaving close of hedges with machines or even the removal of hedges to make larger fields, and the making of silage from grass are all against the nesting of many birds. When farmers spray crops it can be harmful to birds and to the bees. Often a bird's food supply is greatly diminished or contaminated by spraying. We need to learn a greater respect for the earth on which we live and to give account to our Creator on our use of his creation. There was no doubt that Neville cared for God's world and for God.

On our homeward journey we stopped to watch four hares racing around a field. When Neville dropped me at the church I wondered if I could capture the same feeling of awe and reverence that he expressed for the Creator. For a good while in a sunlit church I simply rejoiced at being there and knowing that I was in the presence of God the Creator of all things.

There is a great need to learn to be still before God, in the way that Neville and I were before the dipper, waiting with watchful attentiveness. Neville showed me the danger of hyperaction and the need for stillness and peace in my life. A lot of our prayer should be the same quiet waiting upon God as Neville showed before the dipper. After a time of stillness in the love and presence of God, I went home and reread the poem 'Disclosure' by Ann Lewin.

> Prayer is like watching for the
> Kingfisher. All you can do is
> Be where he is likely to appear, and
> Wait.
> Often nothing much happens;
> There is space, silence and
> Expectancy.
> No visible sign, only the
> Knowledge that he has been there
> And may come again.
> Seeing or not seeing cease to matter,
> You have been prepared.
> But sometimes, when you've almost
> Stopped expecting it,
> A flash of brightness
> Gives encouragement.
>
> (*Watching for the Kingfisher*, 2004, p. 29)

Neville showed me again a challenge to our consumer society. We are not made to possess as much as to be possessed: not to own but to be enraptured by what is around us. So many of us in the hurly-burly of life have lost any sense of wonder or enthusiasm. We treat too many things as mere objects for our use and entertainment and then willingly cast them aside as we move on to something else. Rarely do we get joy from the objects that are around us. We need to learn to enthuse in the world around us and to let each subject 'speak' in its own way. In the play *Look Back in Anger* Jimmy Porter makes a cry from the heart:

> How I long for just a little ordinary, human enthusiasm. Just enthusiasm, that's all. I want to hear a warm thrilling voice cry out 'Hallelujah! Hallelujah! I'm alive' . . . Oh brother it's such a long time since I was with anyone who got enthusiastic about anything.
>
> (John Osborne, 1957)

How often I have applied those words to church services and to Christians in their work. When you realize the word 'enthusiasm' comes from the Greek *en theou* meaning 'in God' it becomes all the more challenging. The great joy of believers is to know and show that we dwell in him and he in us and this in its turn makes us enthusiastic for all that there is.

There have been beautiful days when the sun filled the church with light, the hymns were joyous and I said to the congregation, 'Lift up your hearts.' You might think it would be easy. Back came a dull and half-hearted response: 'We lift them to the Lord.' Looking towards the congregation, there did not seem to be many signs of enthusiasm; most seemed to be very earthbound. There is not a lot of enthusiasm around to inspire us. It is for this reason when I find someone who is enthusiastic I enjoy their company and what they have to show me.

If we do not have enthusiasm during the week for each other and for all of creation we will not be able to fabricate it on a Sunday for worship. We need to move from a society that sees things as dispensable and disposable to one that once again has reverence and respect for what is around us. In a throwaway society there is the danger that people and relationships become as disposable as empty cartons. If we want to know the Creator we need to learn to care for what he has created. We need to see how all things are linked together and the destruction of any creature can diminish us. It does matter if songbirds no longer sing over our fields and if certain species are disappearing for ever. In our modern living many people have been too far removed from the world that sustains us and upon which we depend. Sadly I meet many worshippers who are almost world-denying. If 'God so loved the world' we who are created in his image should show our love for it. We need to show respect and care for the ecosystem on which our lives depend. We should be deeply concerned at the destruction of rain forests and the loss of many creatures. We should seek fair trade for all, standing against injustice and anything that impoverishes people. Yet some church people talk as if it did not matter that the world is being destroyed and abused. It is as if they did not belong to it. There is a type of 'other-worldliness' that forgets that it is God who has given us this world. This is the only world God has given to us and how can we seek another if we do not appreciate this one?

There is something wrong with Christians and their theology that makes them think they can approach the mystery of God without a feeling of reverence and awe for the deep mystery of what he has made. One of the great traps for the person who decides to pray is to turn their back on the world. If our attitude to the world is wrong so will our attitude to its Creator be wrong. I have met many scientists who have a greater sense of awe and wonder towards the world than many churchgoers. I have found the same sense of wonder and respect in bird-watchers, like Neville, in gardeners, artists, poets, and in ecologists that you get from the scientist. It is only those who imagine themselves to be religious that treat the whole of creation with contempt beyond belief. The problem has always been the same. There is always the danger of turning our backs on the world as if it belonged to the enemy. A cautionary tale comes from the life of the abbess Samthann, who ruled the monastery at Clonbroney in Ireland and who died in 739.

> A certain teacher came to the abbess and said: 'I propose to give up study and to give myself to prayer.'
>
> Samthann replied, 'What then can steady your mind and prevent it from wandering, if you neglect study?'
>
> The teacher was obviously in a dissatisfied mode and continued, 'I wish to go abroad on pilgrimage to find God.'
>
> Samthann firmly replied, 'If God cannot be found on this side of the sea, by all means let us all journey overseas. But since God is near to all those who call upon him, we have no need to cross overseas. The kingdom of heaven can be reached from every land.'

Not only was permission refused but also the teacher would have to learn that God was there in the world around him. A medieval Celtic verse said,

> Pilgrim, take care your journey's not in vain,
> a hazard without profit, without gain;
> the King you seek you'll find in Rome, it's true
> but only if he travels on the way with you.

We all need to discover on our journey through this world that the God whom we seek presents himself to us at every moment.

A woman from the island of Harris who suffered from a form of leprosy and collected shellfish from the shore expressed this in a wonderful way:

> There is no plant in all the ground
> But is full of his virtue,
> There is no form in the strand
> But is full of his blessing
> Jesu! Jesu! Jesu!
> Jesu! meet it were to praise him.
>
> There is no life in the sea,
> There is no creature in the river,
> There is naught in the firmament,
> But proclaims his goodness.
> Jesu! Jesu! Jesu!
> Jesu! meet it were to praise him.
>
> There is no bird on the wing,
> There is no star in the sky,
> There is nothing beneath the sun,
> But proclaims his goodness.
> Jesu! Jesu! Jesu!
> Jesu! meet it were to praise him.
>
> (Carmichael, 1983, p. 231)

It would do many Christians good to affirm their own link with the earth and how they depend upon it. Perhaps they should recite as part of a creed the words from 'The Deer's Cry', which is attributed to St Patrick:

> I arise today
> Through the strength of heaven:

Light of sun,
Radiance of moon,
Splendour of fire,
Speed of lightning,
Swiftness of wind,
Depth of sea,
Stability of earth,
Firmness of rock.

(*Selections of Ancient Irish Poetry*, 1928, pp. 25–6)

In the Church in Celtic lands there was often talk of playing the five-stringed harp. This was a proper instrument and has its mention in the Scriptures. It was also an invitation to use the five senses in all that we do. We may play some notes less than others but all need be involved. It is only when we are using our senses and being alert to what is around us that the sixth sense, the 'seeing with the heart' comes into play.

Neville challenges our vision of life and our involvement with the world and with other people. Let us learn to be alert and as attentive as he is. The giving of attention is the giving of your self to the other and so is an act of love.

The story of Moses and the burning bush (Exodus 3.1–6) cannot be understood by the mind but can be known by all who come quietly into the presence or are suddenly aware of God. Moses had run away from Egypt and the court of Pharaoh for he had killed an Egyptian. Moses was in the desert looking after sheep and moving from place to place. He suddenly became aware of something wonderful, the burning bush. We will never know quite what was happening but it confronted Moses with mystery and awe and led him to an awareness of God. He discovered the place on which he stood was holy ground. God is in the world or, to be more theologically correct, the world is in God, and the world waits for us to come in awe before its Creator. We need to discover we are on holy ground, for the earth is the Lord's and all that is in it.

Exercises and reflections

1 Pray

> Lord, I look for you, I long for you.
> I watch for you, I wait for you.
> Come, Lord, open my eyes to your presence.
> Come, Lord, open my ears to your calling.
> Come, Lord, open my heart to your love.

2 Rest, Read, Ruminate, Reflect, React

Rest   in the love and light of the Lord. Know that you need not do anything for God to love you. He has loved you for always. Relax in his presence as you would as if you were sunbathing. There is nothing you need do to let God's love pour into you. Let go of all tension and trouble. Let your mind and your body relax. You may like to concentrate the mind on a beautiful scene. See yourself as there and know that God is with you.

Read   the story of Simeon in Luke 2.25–35

Ruminate   Chew over the story. Think yourself into this scene. See how many of your senses you can involve in visualizing the event. Joseph and Mary had brought the infant Jesus to the Temple to give thanks for his life and for a safe birth as the firstborn. This is a ritual that every Jewish family would perform. There in the Temple was Simeon who believed that he would not die until he had seen the Messiah that is the Christ. All Jews believed that the Messiah would

12

come and redeem his people. Many believed he would come and drive out the enemy, at that time the Romans, and lead them to victory. The Messiah was thought of as a champion of their cause, a king like David who would defeat their enemies. In many ways they were always in danger of seeking someone who would do what they want. In contrast to these there were those who were known as the 'Quiet in the Land'. They looked for the coming of the Messiah and did not think of him conquering peoples or doing what they wished. They quietly watched and waited for his coming; they looked and longed for the coming of God into their lives. Simeon was such a person; he waited for the coming and for the consolation of Israel.

Mary's life is full of wonder yet she must have been surprised when Simeon came forward and asked to hold Jesus. The eyes of the old man must have been bright with joy. Simeon held him in his arms and praised God, saying, 'Master, now you are dismissing your servant in peace, according to your word; for my eyes have seen your salvation' (Luke 2.29–30).

Reflect What had Simeon seen? A little child held in his mother's arms, an infant in all his weakness and vulnerability. Simeon saw further for he saw the Christ. He saw the One who was to be a light to lighten the Gentiles and who was for the glory of Israel. He saw with the eyes of his heart. He saw deeper than others who were passing by and he concentrated his whole attention on this child; his love went out to the Messiah and to his God.

We often fail to see because we do not look close enough or long enough at anything to discover its mystery and wonder. The writer of *The Cloud of Unknowing* says: 'He cannot be comprehended by our intellect, or any man's – or

13

any angel's for that matter. For both they and we are created beings. But only to our intellect is He incomprehensible, not to our love' (*The Cloud of Unknowing*, 1961, ch. 4).

The poet and theologian Teilhard de Chardin says:

> We have only to go a little beyond the frontier of sensible appearances in order to see the divine welling through . . . By means of created things, without exception, the divine assails us, penetrates us, and moulds us. We imagine it as distant and inaccessible, whereas we live steeped in its burning layers. *In eo vivimus.* As Jacob said, awakening from his dream, the world, this palpable world, which we were wont to treat with the boredom and disrespect with which we regard places with no sacred association for us, is in truth a holy place, and we did not know it.
>
> (Teilhard de Chardin, 1975, p. 112)

We have to ask ourselves, do we really give attention to the mystery and the wonders that are about us?

React How open are you to the daily wonders and mysteries that present themselves to you?

Seek to give your full attention to the present moment and all that is in it.

Concentrate on something with undivided attention.

Enjoy being part of the world that is steeped in the Presence.

3 Pray

Wilt thou not visit me?
The plant beside me feels thy gentle dew,

And every blade of grass I see
From thy deep earth its quickening moisture drew.

Wilt thou not visit me?
Thy morning calls on me with cheering tone;
And every hill and tree
Lend but one voice – the voice of thee alone.

Come, for I need thy love,
More than the flower the dew, or grass the rain;
Come, gently as thy holy dove;
And let me in thy sight rejoice to live again.

(Jones Very, 1813–80, quoted in
The SPCK Book of Christian Prayer, 1995)

Love Changes Everything

Once a week I used to spend a day or an afternoon in a local psychiatric hospital. My primary aim was to visit people from the parish. I met a good few people that I knew and over weeks of visiting I got to know many more. Some of the people got few visitors and they looked forward to anyone calling whom they thought they knew. I realized that many lonely and shy people found the ward a giver of security and where they could get a little attention. It is amazing how many people there are that feel deprived of love and understanding and need to know that someone somewhere cares for them. Often a prolonged stay on the ward was like being given a sense of sanctuary, a 'Linus blanket' which they become afraid to do without. There was a great need to encourage people to extend themselves and to learn to trust the world beyond the ward, tough though it may be. They needed to be able to live without the prop of the ward and the nurses but with the knowledge that such a support team was there and ready to help.

As people, we all need the support of others in our lives. Ideally it should come from our family and friends, from teachers and people within our community. We all need to be affirmed in our abilities and encouraged when we have failed; we need to know that we are loved whatever state we are in. Unfortunately so many people lack this early love and encouragement and they become afraid to venture, sometimes afraid to go out or to move on. Too often people receive criticism or cautionary advice when they should be encouraged to adventure. The timid suffer in particular. Many are caught between the dream of venturing and the fear of making mistakes and being rejected or criticized. So they do not venture but live in what has been called 'shadowland'.

I discovered many a lovely person who was said to be having a 'breakdown'. These were not inadequate people or deficient in any way; rather they had come to a new turning in their lives and were finding it difficult to face. Sometimes it was a high-powered business person, who was a workaholic and needed to learn how to rest. This was not so much a breakdown but a suffering from physical and emotional exhaustion. To learn to be still and to meditate would greatly help such a person in his or her life. It is also important to know that we cannot live in our own strength alone.

There was a young woman who had been offered a new and high-powered job and who had shrunk away at the thought. I explored with her the idea that 'breakdown' was often the refusal or the inability to accept our place in a moving world. Often it was not a breakdown but a clampdown on new feelings and experiences. This arose from a desire to live in the past and often under the false idea that the past was better. It was a refusal to change and to be changed. Time and again you hear people say, 'We have not done it that way and we are not going to start now.' Not only people, but also nations, institutions, businesses and churches suffer from clampdown. We need to learn when things are no longer usable. I kept an old lawn-mower for years. I took it to bits every time it broke down. I spent hours tinkering with the engine. I refused to acknowledge it needed renewing. I wasted hours and caused myself much frustration before the mower finally packed up. If I had got rid of it years before I would have been far better off. I know that none of us is free from clampdown in some areas of our lives and this can use up so much energy without us even noticing. We need to know when we have outgrown certain jobs or attitudes. We can do with this as we do with clothes, and we need to be able to change, though many of us need to be encouraged and know we have a support system before we can launch ourselves into the new.

The more I heard of breakdowns the more I wanted to say they were really more often a breakthrough that we were refusing. The events of life are often calling upon us to change, and to improve our lot. Through fear of the unknown, through an attachment to what has been we are unable to move on. Often our past vibrates too strongly in the present. We can spend a good deal of life being unwilling to let go of the past: what has been is strong and often prevents us from moving forward. The old life clings to us tightly around us. I would like everyone to have the experience of the hymn writer John Keble who wrote:

> New every morning is the love
> our wakening and uprising prove;
> through sleep and darkness safely brought,
> restored to life and power and thought.
>
> New mercies, each returning day,
> hover around us while we pray;
> new perils past, new sins forgiven,
> new thoughts of God, new hopes of heaven.

If only it were so easy, but there is a lot of untested truth there.

On one of my visits to the hospital, I received a wonderful compliment from a woman who suffered from schizophrenia. I had spent a lot of time with her over the months and she said to me: 'What I really like about you, you are just like us.' I am glad that she was able to recognize our common humanity and that I could easily have also been admitted! I am sure she would have understood the incarnation of Christ and his coming among us.

On one such visit to the hospital I met Grace. I had known her since she was a child. As she grew up she was an absolute beauty. She had raven-black hair, and skin as white as snow. Her cheeks were a rosy red. I used to look into her dark eyes and know whom she reminded me of, it was Snow White. I thought of her as a picture of health and happiness, though I did remember there was a time when she struggled at school. This was just put down to her growing up.

I was most surprised to see Grace on the ward and she looked a sorry sight. Since I last saw her, the bloom had gone from her cheeks. Her hair was coming out in handfuls. She was suffering from alopecia. This disease of the autoimmune system is often caused when the person is suffering from stress. She had two more 'A's she was suffering from: anorexia and asthma. This frail creature looked as if she was fading away. At first I was not sure she was pleased to see me. The eyes seemed to flash a warning 'unexploded bomb'. I knew I would have to tread carefully if I were to journey at all. Grace was obviously a wounded creature who cried out, 'Do not touch. It hurts!' The pain had centred her on herself and she was unable or unwilling to come out of this shell of protection. She was afraid to face life in its fullness. We talked only of pleasantries and of the nice things I knew she had once enjoyed. I told her I would come again in a week or so.

I met Grace for many weeks and it took all of them before she felt confident in my presence. One day I knew when she was going to tell me something special because she stopped looking at me and looked downwards at the ground. I could see there was great hurt and the need for healing. All her body was crying out in pain. She probably thought she was beyond tears but her whole body was weeping. I had wondered what she had done but never probed. As the story unfolded I saw it was not so much what Grace had done as what had been done to her. My 'Snow White' had been poisoned not by a wicked queen but by a feckless father.

Grace's home life had not been as I had thought. Her father, who was apparently a nice man, had regularly abused Grace since she was quite young. It was only when she got into her teens and threatened to tell others that he stopped. In the normal run of things, Grace would never have told anyone because she knew it would have broken her mother's heart. While at home she kept a chair propped against the door to keep her father out. When she got an opportunity to leave home and work in a neighbouring town she took it. Now she was incredibly lonely. She was afraid of making relationships and she felt like 'soiled goods'. The pain of knowing that her father could have done this to her was eating her away. She was full of anger, sorrow and shame. Her life had been destroyed. How could she ever have an ordinary relationship? The pain of this made her turn more and more in on herself and in many ways she seemed to be fading away. The three 'A's all surfaced almost at once: alopecia, asthma and anorexia. Her work suffered and she had to leave her employment. She saw the doctor and he sent her to a psychiatrist who suggested she be admitted into hospital. Grace seemed to be perishing. Her life was being diminished day by day. All of her energies were spent on keeping the lid on what had happened. Grace badly needed people she could trust and talk to and who would care for her beyond a professional relationship. Grace needed loving but it would have to have a very gentle and deeply caring approach. The two sentences that kept coming to my mind were the refrain of St Paul in his letter to the Corinthians, 'without love I am nothing' (see 1 Corinthians 13.1–3) and the words from St John's

Gospel, 'God so loved the world that he gave his only Son, so that everyone who believes in him may not perish' (John 3.16), though I did not verbally relate these Scriptures to Grace. I expressed no shock at what had happened to her but sought to share in her sorrow. She wept as she told her story and for a good time afterwards. I reached out for her hands and just held them. There were no words, no easy 'absolutions', just an attempt to be there with her in the pain.

The next time I visited Grace she was very nervous. She wanted to be assured I had told no one and that I still had respect for her. I had not mentioned it to a soul, though she had often been in my mind and heart. I continued to visit her on a regular basis and tried to let her see she was cared for but in many ways I felt inadequate. It needed more than me.

Before I ever started to visit her, Grace had met almost daily with a young man who was working in the hospital. He was not part of the nursing staff but was a carer and a gentle soul. He brought Grace books to read and told her of films he had seen. He talked of what was going on outside the hospital. Then he began to bring her little gifts, chocolates and flowers. She got great joy out of both of these, more from saying who had brought them than the things in themselves. In his visits, the carer always trod very carefully. He understood she felt damaged and he did not want to hurt her any more. After a while, they started walking out together within the grounds of the hospital. It was at about this stage Grace's hair began to grow properly again; she was no longer losing hair. She began to eat properly and a new bloom was in her cheeks. Even her asthma abated. Something was happening to Grace that medicine and consultations could not achieve. When a film that Grace badly wanted to see was on at the local cinema she was allowed to go and her new friend took her. On another occasion he took her out for a meal. At the time he did not realize that she had never been taken out for a meal before. Grace had found someone who loved her and yet who made no demands. Grace was loved and in love and this love performed a miracle.

Suddenly the world that she feared had changed. Grace was well enough to leave the hospital and to return to her flat. She started working for a local firm. But the joy of her life was the visits from her newly found friend. He had the sense to treat Grace with great care and respect. He introduced her to others and soon they had a good few friends in common. It was quite a while before they got engaged and then married. It was a lot longer still before their first child was born. Grace had entered again the world of the living, and glowed with the fact that she was loved. The first time I heard the Andrew Lloyd Webber song 'Love changes everything' I thought of Grace.

How like Grace we all are. We need to know we are loved and to be able to love. If we are deprived of that love or that love comes in a debased form it can scar us for life. If an infant is left too long without care and attention it will begin to panic, for this is a matter of life or death. In the same way in later life panic attacks will come upon people who are made to wait too long. We need to know that someone actually cares about us and in fact loves us.

In an ideal world we get love in the earliest stages from our home, our parents and our sisters and brothers. It is for this we are made, to love and to be loved. In many ways we can start loving only after love has been poured into our lives. It is love that gives us a feeling of well-being and security. Love makes us able to venture and to look beyond ourselves. To have been truly loved gives us a power to face anything whereas without it we can easily perish. In the story of *Harry Potter and the Philosopher's Stone*, Quirrell, who is working for the wicked Voldemort, tries to kill Harry but is unable to do so even when he uses all the evil powers available to him. Harry asks:

'Why couldn't Quirrell touch me?'

'Your mother died to save you. If there is one thing
Voldemort cannot understand, it is love . . . Love as power-
ful as your mother's for you leaves its own mark. Not a
visible sign . . . to have been loved so deeply, even though
the person who loved us is gone, will give us some protection for ever.'

(J. K. Rowling, 1997)

To have been loved is like a reservoir that feeds our life. If it has
been denied we are likely to wither and perish. St Paul knew
this well and would say more than once to the Corinthians,
'without love I am nothing' (see 1 Corinthians 13.2, 4). To go
through life without knowing we are loved is to live as deprived
and underdeveloped people. In his first Epistle, St John wants
us to know that we are loved. He wants us to know that whatever is going on God loves us. He says, 'In this is love, not that
we loved God but that he loved us' (1 John 4.10 – it is good to
read all of 1 John 4.7–12). God's love for us is active towards us
before we ever turn to him and God does not stop loving us
whatever we do. Yet it will be difficult for anyone to experience
the love of God without that love being revealed through
another person. For Grace, the image of a loving father was not
one she could easily accept. Grace survived those difficult times
because she realized just how much her mother loved her.
It was through her mother's love that she would be able to
experience and trust other loves.

Ours is not an ideal world and love is tainted like everything
else. Love comes from human beings who are not perfect and
who often make mistakes. For us all, between the ideal and the
reality falls the shadow. Love is sometimes denied us and at
other times offered in a distorted form. Smother love can pro-
tect us and possess us in ways that are not good for our growth

24

or our well-being. Love can threaten by saying, 'If you do that I will not love you.' True love can never say that and we should never say it. We need to show that some things will hurt us deeply if our beloved does them, but true love will not cease to love. It is said of God he does not love the sin but loves the sinner and we are to reflect such love as well as we can. Yet in our world love is often given with terms and conditions – that is not love in its fullness, though many realize that the danger of unconditional love is that it can crucify us. Again we show in this we are made in the image of God.

Sadly none of us comes through life unscathed. We discover that love can easily be betrayed, misused or abused. To be abused by an enemy or a stranger is something we may learn to come to terms with but when abused by a loved one it is very hard to bear. Jesus is not the only one who was betrayed with a kiss. A MORI survey of 2,019 adults showed that at least 10 per cent of them had suffered from at least one sexually abusive experience before the age of 16. That was allowing only for those who could admit it and not for those who had deeply repressed it in their minds. Sex and love are often confused because sex can be a great expression of love. But if we are abused then that is never an expression of love. This can leave us damaged for the rest of our lives. It is only the self-giving love of another that can redeem many of the situations we find ourselves in.

Love really does change everything. It changes the way we look at each other, the way we look at life and the way we understand who we are. Love is very often redemptive. George Herbert expresses this well in his poem on love.

> Love bade me welcome, yet my soul drew back.
> Guilty of dust and sin.
> But quick-eyed Love, observing me grow slack

From my first entrance in,
Drew nearer to me, sweetly questioning
If I lacked anything.

'A guest', I answered, 'worthy to be here.'
Love said, 'You shall be he.'
'I, the unkind, the ungrateful? Ah, my dear.
I cannot look on thee.'
Love took my hand and smiling did reply,
'Who made the eye but I?'

'Truth, Lord, but I have marred them, let my shame
Go where it doth deserve.'
'And know you not', says Love, 'who bore the blame?'
'My dear then I will serve.'
'You must sit down', says Love, 'and taste my meat.'
So did I sit and eat.

(George Herbert, 1593–1633)

Love will not force itself upon us but will invite us to experience it and to be transformed by it. In this we need to trust love, even in this fallen world. If we are fortunate enough we will meet at least one person with whom we can truly share our love. Then the love that is poured into our lives can be released and poured out towards others. The strange thing about love is the more you give it away the more it grows. Love is not for self but for an outpouring of self towards others. Love turns us away from ourselves and helps us to look outward and beyond the confines of our own space. More than this there is something eternal about real love. This makes St John say: 'Beloved, let us love one another, because love is from God; everyone who loves is born of God and knows God. Whoever does not love does not know God, for God is love (1 John

4.7–8). Elizabeth Barrett Browning (1806–61) expresses this beautifully in:

A Wife to a Husband

How do I love thee? Let me count the ways.
I love thee to the depth and breadth and height
My soul can reach, when feeling out of sight
For the end of Being and ideal Grace.
I love thee to the level of everyday's
Most quiet need, by sun and candlelight.
I love thee freely, as men strive for right;
I love thee purely, as they turn from praise.
I love thee with the passion put to use
In my old griefs, and with my childhood's faith.
I love thee with a love I seemed to lose
With my lost saints, – I love thee with the breath,
Smiles, tears, of all my life! – and, if God choose,
I shall but love thee better after death.

Grace was fortunate enough to have someone who was willing to love her for who she really was and not for some ideal or for ideas of changing her or making her different. Yet in that love Grace was transformed. I am sure it was never easy or straightforward. There would be many difficult moments and times of retreating but love accepted this and pouring love in made it possible for love to be outpoured.

In the Old Testament Hosea had a hard time. To be a prophet and speak against the unfaithfulness of Israel was hard enough but Hosea also had an unfaithful wife. Gomer went off more than once. Hosea did not cease to love her. When Gomer was sold into slavery Hosea redeemed her. As his wife had deserted him and was unfaithful, Hosea saw that this was often our relationship to the God who loves us. We chase after other loves and forsake the God who loves us with an everlasting love. God seeks to restore the breakdown in our relationships. Hosea realized God did not want gifts, sacrifices or burnt offerings; more than things God wants us and our love: 'For I desire steadfast love and not sacrifice, the knowledge of God rather than burnt-offerings' (Hosea 6.6). Jeremiah would continue this idea of God's love when he has God say, 'I have loved you with an everlasting love; therefore I have continued my faithfulness to you' (Jeremiah 31.3).

Exercises and Reflections

1 Pray

> *O Deus, ego amo te*
>
> O God, I love thee, I love thee –
> Not out of hope of heaven for me
> Nor fearing not to love and be
> In everlasting burning.
> Thou, thou, my Jesus, after me
> Didst reach thine arms out dying,
> For my sake sufferedst nails and lance,
> Mocked and marrèd countenance,
> Sorrows passing number,
> Sweat and care and cumber,
> Yea and death, and this for me,
> And thou couldst see me sinning:
> Then I, why should I not love thee,
> Jesu, so much in love with me?
> Not for heaven's sake; not to be
> Out of hell by loving thee;
> Nor for any gains I see;

But just the way that thou didst me
I do love and will love thee;
What must I love thee, Lord, for then?
For being my king and God. Amen.

(Gerard Manley Hopkins, 1844–89)

2 Rest, Read, Ruminate, Reflect, React

Rest in the love of God. Know that God loves you and is with you. Make sure that your body is not tense. Seek to relax each part in turn starting at your feet and moving up until you reach your neck and head. Let the mind relax. Picture a calm lake and see yourself at the edge. Know that, as you look upon its calmness, God is with you and offers you his love and peace.

Read Luke 7.36–50

Ruminate Chew over the events. Jesus has been asked out to a meal. One of the Pharisees has invited him. This is a good-living and a 'righteous' man. Others have come to hear and to see the celebrity Jesus. The scene is set in a courtyard and perhaps a fountain is flowing. As guests arrive, they are given the kiss of peace by their host. This would not be omitted in the case of a respected teacher. Each has cool water poured over his or her feet to wash away the dust of the road. Then often a sweet-smelling drop of attar of roses was sprinkled on the head. It would appear that Jesus was given none of these courtesies. The table was a low one at which guests reclined and their feet stretched out away from the table. Into this situation comes a woman and she stands behind Jesus. He is aware of her hot tears falling on his feet. But he does not move. The woman bends down to wipe his feet with her loose hair. Loose hair was seen to be the signs of a loose woman!

Jesus feels her hair and her hands on his feet and does not move away. She starts to put perfume on his feet. The room is filled with the smell. The Pharisee found the whole act outrageous and said to himself, 'If this man were a prophet, he would have known who and what kind of woman is touching him – she is a sinner.' Jesus no doubt knew and his love still went out towards her. The Pharisee could not easily receive the love of Jesus because of his judgemental and righteous attitudes. In Jesus the woman found acceptance and forgiveness. In the love of Jesus her life was renewed and given a chance to be different. But Jesus loved her as she was, not as he or anyone wanted her to be. In the same way in the story of the Prodigal Son, the wayward youth is forgiven. The one who stands on rights and deserts is offered the same love but finds it hard to accept it (read Luke 15.11–32).

Reflect Know that you are loved as you are. God made us all different, and he loves each of us in our uniqueness. God loves you for yourself and not for the potential that is yours, though his love often frees people to fulfil their potential. Julian of Norwich says of God: 'In his love he wraps us and holds us. He enfolds us for love, and he will never let us go.' Julian also says:

Full lovingly does our Lord hold us when it seems to us we are nearly forsaken and cast away because of our sin – and deservedly so.

Our courteous Lord does not want his servants to despair even when they fall often and grievously into sin. For our falling does not hinder him from loving us.

This is princely friendship from our courteous Lord
and he still sustains us secretly even while we are in sin.
He touches us gently and shows us our sin by the kindly
light of mercy and grace.

(Julian of Norwich, 1980, p. 18)

React Are you aware that God's love enfolds you, that God
accepts you as you are? You are in the heart of God and God
seeks to be within your heart. He will not force himself upon
you. You can keep him out by your own self-righteousness
or by your straying away in sin. You can remain outside by
your own hard standards. But God is waiting for you to come
to him.

Promise yourself that you will spend a part of each day
acknowledging God's love. You may like to remember the
words of St Augustine of Hippo: 'You have made us for yourself, and our heart is restless till it finds its rest in you.'

We have to ask ourselves, do we truly know that our God
loves us? We need daily give thanks for all who love us and to
give our love to them.

3 Pray for those who have suffered from abuse.

Jesus, our brother and friend,
look with kindness and compassion
on those who are sexually abused.
You see the lost child within
still crying alone in the darkness
where the hidden wounds of childhood
still hurt and make them feel afraid.
When they feel abandoned, give them hope,
when they feel ashamed, give them comfort,
when they feel unloved, give them faith,

when they feel betrayed, give them peace.
In the power of your resurrection
may love triumph over fear,
light shine in the darkness,
and the long reign of terror be ended.

(Hansen, 1991, pp. 39–40)

Glory to God in the Highest

It was a cold winter's morning with icy roads and difficult travelling. There was a good turnout at the service in the small country church. The inside of the church was no warmer than the outside, though it was a refuge from the wind. It was after nearly everyone else had left that I met Walter. His suit looked as if it had been made 20 years earlier. Yet it was well pressed and he was tidily dressed. From the moment he shook hands I was aware of his eyes, for he could not see properly. Walter gave me a friendly welcome and told me that his job each Sunday was pumping the organ and making sure the bellows were full for the organist to play properly. He sensed the amount of air needed, as he could not see the gauge, and the organ never faltered. I discovered later that the organ could easily have been put on to an electric blower but out of deference for Walter it was left as it was made, to be hand-pumped.

I would see Walter at his station Sunday by Sunday, sitting quietly at least 20 minutes before the service and then working his way through the hymns. I learnt that Walter walked to church and back home after each service, a round trip of about three miles, though when the weather was wet or snowy, Walter usually accepted a lift. Once a good few years back he and his mother had moved away from the village to another village seven miles away. Walter still came to the service and walked the seven miles there and seven miles back. He said it was a joy to be out and on the country roads, though he did admit that he often got a lift home. I was to discover he was a very determined and independent person and did not like to feel he was dependent on others.

In time I got to know Walter well. He lived with his mother in a small cottage. His father had died many years ago. The cottage was always cosy with a good fire burning next to the oven that was used for cooking. There was always good, wholesome, home-made food and the smell of baking often filled the little house. The house could have done with a renovation but both were content with their lot. In the evenings they often listened to a talking book on a tape recorder, though both enjoyed a good deal of silence. Walter could get about without help. He did not use a white stick to declare his difficulty in seeing. He said it was just as if he was walking in a fog all the time; he could not see anything with a clear outline. Though not educated he was no one's fool and full of country wisdom. His sense of hearing in some ways compensated for his poor sight. He rejoiced in the sounds of the birds and could tell each one by its sound. He was not much of a talker but often his silence spoke louder than a string of words. As he got older I persuaded him that he should have a lift to the service and another home. I knew I was on dangerous ground but as the journey was getting too hard for him he relented.

There was one area where I made a mistake and was corrected by him in his own inimitable way. After many visits to their home I realized that he and his mother lived on a very tight budget. A little more money would not have come amiss. One day as I drove him to his home, I suggested that could we pay him for the work he did. I was careful to point out that I was paid for taking services. By the silence that followed I knew I had offended him. Yet I had suggested it because I thought it might have been helpful. When we arrived at his door Walter did not get out of the car. He had obviously been thinking how to reply to me without offending me. In his usual courteous way he thanked me for my kind offer. It was good of me to think he might like being paid. Then he continued in a quiet voice,

How can you pay me for giving to God what I can? I pump the organ for the glory of God and not for a reward. We do not have much money, so this is my way of giving. I walked to church for years to give glory to him. Every stroke in pumping of the organ I give glory to him. You cannot pay me for that for I already have my reward. I do it for the glory of God. Thank you again for your kind offer but there is no need.

With that he got out of the car and went into his house. I sat outside for a moment or two, greatly humbled. I had been given a glimpse of love and dedication. Walter sought to give glory to the God whom he worshipped. He saw more clearly than many people that you cannot cost out some acts and that financial reward is only a secondary result if it is required at all. I was aware that I had shared the journey with a contented and a very dedicated man.

'I do it for the glory of God' – this refrain of Walter's went with me for the rest of the day if not for ever. Walter had a simple relationship with the ever-present God that enriched his life and gave it more meaning and purpose, which many have never found. As I moved away from his house a poem of Gerard Manley Hopkins came to mind, 'The Candle Indoors':

Some candle clear burns somewhere I come by . . .
There/ God to aggrandise, God to glorify.

Walter was such a burning light and a witness to the presence of God in his life and in the ordinary daily tasks he did. I went home and read again part of an address that Gerard Manley Hopkins had written on *The Spiritual Exercises of Ignatius Loyola*:

> Begin to give God glory. The moment we do this we reach the end of our being, we do what we were made for, we make it worth God's while to have created us . . .
>
> Turn then, brethren, now and give God glory. You do say grace at meals and thank and praise God for your daily bread, so far so good, but thank and praise him now for everything. When a man is in God's grace and free from mortal sin, then everything that he does, so long as there is no sin in it, gives God glory, and what does not give him glory has some, however little, sin in it. It is not only prayer that gives God glory but work. Smiting on an anvil, sawing a beam, whitewashing a wall, driving horses, sweeping, scouring, everything gives God some glory if being in his grace you do it as your duty. To go to communion worthily gives God great glory, but to take food in thankfulness and temperance gives him glory too. To lift up the hands in prayer gives God glory, but a man with a dungfork in his hand, a woman with a sloppail, give him glory too. He is so great that all things give him glory if you mean they should. So then, my brethren live.
>
> (*Gardner*, 1953, p. 144)

Walter had an awareness of the presence of God that would put many preachers and scholars into the shade. He saw far more clearly than many with 20/20 vision. Some would call his attitude simplistic if not downright simple, but it helped him to see his place in the world and gave to his daily routine a sense of meaning, of purpose and of value that so many of us lack today. He saw a world that was full of the presence of God, and his simplest of tasks as God-related. In a strange way I saw the link between Walter and the visionary poet Edwin Muir. In the churchyard where Edwin Muir is buried at Swaffham Prior there are words on his gravestone that he had chosen himself:

> ... his unblinded eyes
> saw far and near
> the fields of Paradise.

In a wonderful way Walter had the 'unblinded eye' of a visionary. If vision is about seeing clearly then Walter saw further and deeper than many who count themselves as perceptive. It was not by chance that the first hymn the following Sunday was 'To God be the glory'. By the big smile on Walter's face I knew it was a comment on what he had said as well as our giving glory to God. Whenever I saw Walter pumping the organ I heard in my mind him saying, 'I do it for the glory of God.'

These were words that vibrated in my life for I had met them many times before. When I was still in my teens I went to train to be a priest at Kelham near Newark in Nottinghamshire. This was at a time when many offering themselves for ministry were renewing the Church and there were many applicants for a few places. I was one of 14 who went there in 1954. The training was done under a monastic discipline led by the Society of the Sacred Mission. Our day would be divided into worship, study, manual work and rest and we were required to do all for the glory of God. When I arrived at Kelham I was given a little book entitled *Principles*. The title page had: 'Fear God and give glory to him; for the hour of His judgement has come.' The next page had only the Society's motto: *Ad Gloriam Dei in eius voluntate*, 'To the Glory of God in doing his will'. The page that was the beginning of the *Principles* began:

I

By this you were created – the Will of God. And to this end – the Praise of His Glory.

II

You will be judged by what you are, and what avail will it be to you at the last, if you have glorified God very little in yourself, that you have talked of His Glory in many lands.

(*Principles*, 1930)

This was all very high-minded stuff for someone who had just come from working in a coal mine. I wondered if I would ever take it in. My learning came from a lay brother within the community. I had the privilege of working with him on quite a few occasions.

He would say,

It is easy. All you have to learn to do is to work for God. Not for wages, not for praise, not for gaining anything. Work knowing you are in the presence of God.

Whatever your task, be it worshipping in the chapel or cleaning out the urinals, do it for the glory of God. That means you will not skimp on attention in chapel or fail to clean around the bend of the urinals!

He said all this with a wicked twinkle in his eye but I knew it was the way he lived. This would slowly transform many things in my life; nothing was dull or ordinary for all had the potential of being done for God's glory. If it could not be done to the glory of God it was likely that it should not be done at all. To live and work to his glory is to acknowledge not only the presence of God but the will of God. To give glory to God is to say, 'Your will be done.' It is not an accident that the glory experienced by Moses in the Old Testament is linked to the giving of the commandments. We cannot seek to give God glory if we are out of harmony with his creation. It is when we seek to care for his world and all that is in it, when we reverence the planet and all its creatures that we can say we are striving to live to his glory. Children often have this sense of awe and reverence in their lives but sadly they lose it as they grow older. Wonder and awe do not seem to be the part of many lives today. The poet Wordsworth expressed sadness at the loss of this awareness in the opening stanzas of his ode, 'Intimations of Immortality':

> There was a time, when meadow, grove, and stream,
> The earth, and every common sight,
> To me did seem
> Apparelled in celestial light,
> The glory and the freedom of a dream.
> It is not now as it hath been of yore;–
> Turn wheresoe'er I may,
> By night or day,
> The things which I have seen I now can see no more.
>
> The rainbow comes and goes,
> and lovely is the rose,
> The moon doth with delight
> Look round her when the heavens are bare;
> Waters on a starry night
> Are beautiful and fair;
> The sunshine is a glorious birth;
> But yet I know, where'er I go,
> That there hath passed away a glory from the earth.

We live in times that can be dangerously bereft of glory. Much of our education system and the attitude of a good deal of modern living seem determined to keep God out of the picture. And with the loss of the awareness of his presence, much of life becomes lonely and dull; we as people lose a radiance that is

41

meant to be ours. Education that fills us with facts but often does not allow us to experience what is around is a poor education indeed and leads many to be bored with so-called learning. We need to keep glory and wonder in our lives as well as bare facts. Without glory our goals can be only short-term at the best and for many without glory life can be seen at the best only like that of the creatures in *Alice in Wonderland*, that is, all slapstick and under the constant threat of death. At the worst, life without glory is just meaningless and trivial.

'Glory' is shorthand for the presence of God; though often hidden by cloud it is a glory that is always there. Glory is something we may get a glimpse of from time to time and yet it underlies all that is. Glory is something we can reflect in our faces, as Moses did when he came down from the mountain, if we are aware of the presence and power of God in our lives and the world. Glory is God's gift of himself to us if we will accept it. 'To do it for God's glory', for the presence that is with us, can totally transform how we see and how we live. George Herbert said this was the elixir that turned everything to gold. His poem entitled 'The Elixir' is often sung in churches.

> Teach me, my God and King,
> In all things thee to see;
> And what I do in anything
> To do it as for thee.
>
> A man that looks on glass,
> On it may stay his eye;
> Or, if he pleaseth, through it pass,
> And then the heaven espy.
>
> All may of thee partake;
> Nothing can be so mean

Which, with this tincture, *For thy sake*,
Will not grow bright and clean.

A servant with this clause
Makes drudgery divine;
Who sweeps a room, as for thy laws,
Makes that and th'action fine.

This is the famous stone,
That turneth all to gold;
For that which God doth touch and own
Cannot for less be told.

(George Herbert, 1593–1633)

To see glory in this way says something about what we believe about God. Our God is not a God who is far off but a God with whom we have to do, a God who is near and ever-present. God is there, waiting for us to meet him. Prayer is not a long-distance call to the beyond but a turning to the presence in our midst. To do it for his glory is to acknowledge God in all that we do. It is not so much what we achieve but the basic reason for why we are doing it that inspires our activities. This faith, this relationship with the living God, in no way diminishes our lives but expands them in ways that know no boundaries. It is this that can make Gerard Manley Hopkins say:

The world is charged with the grandeur of God.
It will flame out, like shining from shook foil.

In the same way Teilhard de Chardin says: 'By means of all created things, without exception, the divine assails us, penetrates us and moulds us. We imagined it as distant and inaccessible, whereas we live steeped in its burning layers' (Teilhard de Chardin, 1975, p. 112). Again he says:

43

God, in all that is most living and incarnate in him is not far away from us, altogether apart from the world we see, touch, hear, smell and taste about us. Rather he awaits us every instant, in our action, in the work of the moment. There is a sense in which he is at the tip of my pen, my spade, my brush, my needle – or my heart and my thought.

(Teilhard de Chardin, 1975, p. 64)

This is a wonderful world full of glory. It is a God-filled world to be enjoyed by those who have eyes to see. Walter and his doing things for God's glory challenged me. I rejoice each time I leave a church service and go out to my daily routine by saying, 'Send us out in the power of your Spirit to live and work to your praise and glory.'

King David's life had many ups and downs, joys and sorrows but in all he was aware of God and his glory. Once established as king, David plans to build a great temple to the glory of God. He regularly puts aside some of his wealth for this project. Before his death he makes a last, lavish, personal offering for the temple building fund (1 Chronicles 29.1–5). His example calls from the people a similar joyful response, and gifts pour in (vv. 6–9). David is deeply moved and gives glory to God that people are able to be so generous, who apart from God's goodness would have had nothing. The prayer he uses is one well worth our use still today:

Blessed are you, O Lord, the God of our ancestor
Israel, for ever and ever.
Yours, O Lord, are the greatness, the power, the
glory, the victory, and the majesty;
for all that is in the heavens and on earth is yours;
yours is the kingdom, O Lord, and you are exalted
as head above all.

Riches and honour come from you, and you rule
   over all.
In your hand is power and might;
and it is in your hand to make great and to give
   strength to all.
And now, our God, we give thanks to you and
   praise your glorious name . . .
For all things come from you, and of your own
   have we given you.

(1 Chronicles 29.10–14)

Exercises and Reflections

1 Pray

> Awaken me Lord
> To your light,
> Open my eyes
> To your presence.
>
> Awaken me Lord.
> To your love,
> Open my heart
> To your indwelling.
>
> Awaken me Lord
> To your life,
> Open my mind
> To your abiding.
>
> Awaken me Lord
> To your purpose,
> Open my will
> To your guiding.

(Adam, 1989, p. 7)

2 Rest, Read, Ruminate, Reflect, React

Rest Still your heart and mind and enjoy the reality that you are in the presence and love of God. God's glory is all about you. Let your body relax in his presence as you would in the sunshine. There is no need for effort, allow it to happen; just make space in your life for his glory. If you find the mind wandering concentrate it on something beautiful God has made, such as a leaf or a flower and give thanks for his glory. Let him speak to you through beauty and mystery.

Read the story of the birth of Ichabod, 1 Samuel 4.19–22

Ruminate Here is a sad story. In the chapter before this we have the call of Samuel and God speaking to him in the temple at Shiloh. The ark of the covenant of the Lord of hosts is at Shiloh. The sons of the priest Eli, Hophni and Phineas, are not going to follow in their father's footsteps and they hold what is sacred lightly. Though the priest's family was entitled to a share of the sacrificial offerings Eli's sons are seizing the best for themselves before the offering was ever given to God. These two are blasphemers who are profiteering out of religion. The ark of the covenant is taken from Shiloh as a rallying point for the battle and Eli's sons are with it. Israel is defeated, the ark taken and Hophni and Phineas are among the slain. When Eli hears of this he falls over backwards off his seat: his neck is broken and he dies. The temple at Shiloh never recovers and was probably destroyed in these battles. During all this the wife of Phineas goes into labour. She gives birth to a son but her own life is ebbing away. The women who attend her try to encourage her and tell her not to be afraid and that she has a son. As she

46

is about to die she calls her son 'Ichabod', which means 'The glory has departed from Israel'. Her thoughts are on the ark of God and the deaths of her father-in-law and her husband. No wonder she felt the glory had gone. Life can be tough and even tougher if we feel we are without God. Perhaps as Phineas did not think much of God, neither did his wife. It is sad to find her thinking she is in such a God-forsaken state. God never leaves us; not even in our deepest troubles.

Reflect We are better to lose a god who is only an idol or of whom we have a poor image or little respect that we may come before the living God. Though all the trappings of religion were destroyed God is not destroyed with them. God is not bound by the images and ideas we have about him. God always cares for his people and for his world.

Our God is with us in the bad times as well as the good. If we fail to seek his glory in the good times then it will be much harder for us to know it in the bad times. It is of the utmost importance that we know that God is with us and that his glory is all about us. Our God is greater than our thoughts, beyond our comprehension, and yet God is always with us and known to us through our hearts.

React Promise that you will seek to live your life and do your work to his glory.

You may like to say each day words of Michelangelo: 'Lord, make me see your glory in every place.'

You may even extend these words to say:

Let me see your glory
In every place and in every face.
Let me seek your glory
In all that I hear and all that I do.

47

Let me see your glory
In each created thing, in its mystery and wonder.
Let me seek your glory in this life and through eternity.

Do you truly realize that the glory of God, his wonderful presence, is always there and this presence has the power to transform all that we do?

3 Pray

May none of God's wonderful works
keep silence, night or morning.
Bright stars, high mountains, the depth of the seas,
sources of rushing rivers:
may all these break into song as we sing
to Father, Son and Holy Spirit.
May all the angels in heaven reply:
Amen! Amen! Amen!
Power, praise, honour, eternal glory
to God the only giver of grace.
Amen! Amen! Amen!

(A prayer from third-century Egypt quoted in
The SPCK Book of Christian Prayer, 1995)

The Eclipse of the Heart

Many artists and photographers came to the island as it has so many good scenes to capture on canvas, sketch pad or camera. Holy Island Castle is one of the great icons of Northumbria and must be one of the most painted and photographed castles in the whole country. Among the artists who came year after year were two close friends. One of them liked painting seascapes and the other painted the castle in all its moods. Both were good at what they did and sold their paintings easily. The paintings of the castle sold very quickly. The friends went into partnership back home in County Durham and opened a small gallery that they shared and paid for out of a common account that they held for this purpose. All seemed to be going really well.

I was surprised when only Jim turned up for their usual fortnight's painting holiday. I was more surprised when I saw his latest painting of the castle. It was well below his usual standard and he knew it. 'This one is destined for the scrap heap, like me,' was his comment on the painting. I knew then there was something wrong. I invited him across to my house for the usual cuppa and without prompting I got the whole story. His friend had met a woman when on a painting holiday in Spain. He had decided to live in Spain. That was all right in itself but he had gone off with the whole of their savings. He had left Jim with bills and hardly any money to pay them. I made little comment but I could see that this had left Jim in a disturbed state. There was a great deal of anger and that was using up an awful lot of Jim's time and energy. Jim felt desolate.

Desolation is something we all experience when an event turns us in on ourselves. It is caused by inner turmoil or by something stealing our energies and demanding attention. Such a feeling cuts us off from friends and even from help. We tend to concentrate on ourselves but do not get pleasure out of what we are doing. We get out of harmony with the world and what is around us. In Jim's case I remembered some words from the days I studied clinical theology, words of Frank Lake, 'Where there is rancour there is torpor.' The anger Jim had towards what his friend had done was absorbing much of his energy and he was finding it hard to concentrate on anything else. Yet these were early days, and I did feel that Jim would come out of this cloud; he was not the sort to stay absorbed in his own troubles.

The next morning was one of those wonderful mornings. Early rain had washed the landscape and it was vibrant with colour in the morning light. Inside St Mary's Church the light was almost tangible. Here at 7.30 a.m. Jim came to Morning Prayer, which was not his usual pattern. Jim gave his attention to the service the same way he would to a painting. There were pieces of the service that touched him and moved him. The following comments are from Jim and me looking again at the service afterwards. One of the opening prayers says: 'As we rejoice in the gift of this new day, so may the light of your presence, O God, set our hearts on fire with love for you; now and for ever.' Jim felt this was especially for him. He needed the transforming power of the love of God to make a change in his life and reactions. He wanted to burn with love and to be rid of the anger.

The first psalm was Psalm 24, which said: 'Who shall ascend the hill of the LORD? And who shall stand in his holy place?

Those who have clean hands and pure hearts' (verses 3 and 4). Jim said this was why he came: for a cleansing of his heart, a washing away of any anger or resentment. 'As I stood there, with the morning light flooding into the church and touching us with colours from the east window. I was aware that I was given the chance of renewal and refreshment.'

The reading from the Old Testament that followed was about Balaam blessing Israel. Twice Balaam is called 'the man whose eye is clear' (Numbers 24.3, 15). Jim said this is something all artists need, if not all people. There is need for a clear eye and not to come to a subject distracted or disgusted with life. The clear eye means we will not impose ourselves on to what we see but let it touch us and move us. I made Jim laugh by telling him that, in this story of Balaam, the ass that carried Balaam had a clearer vision than the prophet!

After the New Testament lesson, which was about Legion, the man possessed by demons (Luke 8.26–39), the response for the congregation to make after this reading was: 'Come Holy Spirit, fill the hearts of your people and kindle in us the fire of your love.' I noticed that Jim said this with some feeling. Jim stayed in church for the Communion Service. When I said, 'Lift up your hearts' I saw Jim looking at me with tears in his eyes.

After this full hour in church Jim came to me before I had put everything away and asked if he could see me after breakfast. This was often the time people caught me and made arrangements to see me. I said, 'Yes' and he came at 9.30 a.m. I could see he was being deeply moved. He told me how each of the readings almost shouted at him that they were asking him to be changed. Each had affected him and in some way he now felt washed clean. With a twinkle in his eye he said, 'I do not know whether it was the light and the stillness, the readings, or God at work.' I asked him why worry, surely it was all of these. God works through the world in which we live. We do not need to ask was it this or that; it was all working together. This was not to forget the input and attention given by Jim himself.

Jim told me more of his story. Since his friend had left he had struggled financially but there was something worse. He said:

> In the words of a popular song I have suffered from a 'total eclipse of the heart'. My heart is numb, turned to stone. No one can touch me or move me. I am dead to the world. I do not see beauty. I do not thrill to the changing light and the dance of colours. I can no longer see with the eye of my heart.

I could see in his face the desolation he felt. Desolation means living without the light, without the sun. I knew what Jim meant by a total 'eclipse of the heart', for that is desolation. This is something we all go through more than once in our life. We turn away from the light or some event clouds the brightness and we walk in darkness. Through my mind for a moment flashed the words of the prophet Isaiah that are usually read near Christmas: 'The people who walked in darkness have seen a great light; those who lived in a land of deep darkness – on them light has shined' (Isaiah 9.2). I had the feeling that for Jim the light was beginning to shine again, that the clouds were dispersing. I felt this because of the way he had reacted to the morning service. It had been far more enlightening to him than it had been to me! Maybe already a new dawn was breaking. If Jim had experienced desolation he was already receiving some consolation.

It is interesting to look at the word 'consolation' for it means 'with the light', travelling with the sun and not against it: working with the light that is given to us. For the Christian that is not only the light of the day but the light of God. There are so many people who complain about darkness and troubles who are actually going against the light, who are working against the grain. We need to learn to live in harmony with the world and with each other if we hope to walk in the light.

The Celtic peoples had words for working with the sun and for working against it. *Deasil* meant working with the sun and not going against it. This was acted out in 'encircling prayers' that they always made in a clockwise direction, that is sun-wise. They encircled themselves by pointing outwards with their right hand and turning in a circle. They also encircled their homes and their cattle by walking around them in prayer. This was no magic, though to the unknowing it could deteriorate into it. It was affirming the presence and the desire to live in harmony with the world. It was not making God come, for that is magic, but acknowledging that God is with us and we can turn to him. Going *deasil* was to acknowledge that God is present and we seek to do his will in the world.

To go 'widdershins' is to go anti-clockwise, that is against the sun. It is interesting how many folk tales talk of the danger of going widdershins. If you do, awful things can happen. Again this is not magic but common sense; if you work against the grain you will find the results harder to obtain and it will be much rougher. To go widdershins is to experience desolation and to be out of harmony with what is around you. There is a way of living in harmony and there is a way of being out of tune. Life is sometimes like joining a dance. You need to learn the steps and you need to get into the rhythm. There are times when you can only watch and wait until you capture the rhythm. If you try and force your way in, it is likely you will tread on someone's toes!

Fortunately I knew Jim well. I knew him to be a sensitive and caring person. In acknowledging his problem I was sure he would reach a solution. We talked about the need for trust and yet also the awareness that our trust can sometimes be ill-founded. If a stranger had taken Jim's money he would have soon forgotten it; that his friend had done it was harder to understand and accept. I checked that Jim was not left bankrupt or unable to cope with his gallery. He said it might be a little tough in the short term but he was still better off than he had been a few years back. At least he had a gallery and an outlet for his work. My only suggestion at this stage was to use the island as a place to relax in and not be tempted to achieve much. I secretly hoped that in the letting go new things might happen to Jim. I hoped that already he was moving into the light.

After he left, three images filled my mind. Had the splinter of glass from the Snow Queen's mirror got into Jim's eye and heart? It sounded like it. But the story of the Snow Queen has a happy ending and Kay is rescued from this distracting and distorting state by the love and care of Gerda. I knew that Jim had a loving family and were supportive in these difficult times.

The other two images came from one of my favourite books, *The Little Prince* by Saint-Exupéry. Both are about roses and both are about seeing. I took my well-used copy down from the shelf and read:

'Good-bye,' said the fox, 'And now here is my secret, a very simple secret: it is only with the heart that one can see rightly; what is essential is invisible to the eye.' The little prince repeated, so that he would be sure to remember.

'It is the time you have wasted for your rose that makes your rose so important.'

'It is the time I have wasted for my rose,' said the little prince, so that he would be sure to remember.

'Men have forgotten this truth,' said the fox. 'But you must not forget it. You have become responsible, forever, for what you have tamed. You are responsible for your rose . . .'

'I am responsible for my rose,' the little prince repeated, so that he would be sure to remember.

(Saint-Exupéry, 1962, p. 84)

The second, a few pages further on, once again speaks of 'looking with the heart':

'The men where you live,' said the little prince, 'raise five thousand roses in the same garden – and they do not find in it what they are looking for!'

'They do not find it,' I replied.

'And yet what they are looking for could be found in one single rose or a drop of water.'

'That is true,' I said.

And the little prince added: 'But the eyes are blind: one must look with the heart.'

(Saint-Exupéry, 1962, pp. 91–2)

Jim was complaining he could not see with the heart. I wondered just how many people ever used this 'sixth sense'. I know he was talking about sensitivity and about seeing things not as objects but as subjects in their own right. For the artist, if not for everyone, it is necessary to be able to look in a relaxed and open way at the subject that is before them: to let the heart go out to it and not impose themselves upon the subject. We come to the present distracted by many thoughts and by our own past experience. We can look with jaundiced eyes that distort all that we see. We carry so much with us when there is need to be able to zoom in and focus on that one thing and on that alone. The artist needs to get to know his subject. If he is to paint it well his heart has to go out to it, he has to love it. In many ways I feel that Augustine of Hippo understood this well. When he talks of our so-called end he says:

All shall be Amen and Alleluia.
We shall rest and we shall see,
We shall see and we shall know,
We shall know and we shall love,
We shall love and we shall praise.
Behold our end which is no end.

There is no doubt that to see properly we need to be relaxed. If we are uptight about life or what we are doing we will not see it in the proper light. We all need to let go of tensions in our lives, the things that distract us and stop us living in the present moment. It is like when we stop searching for a word or name; then it will often come to us. To let the new into our life we have often to let go of what has already been. Too many people are unable to meet the present because of preoccupation. Relax, let go and let your eyes be cleansed. Rest and then you will see.

You will see and you will know. Vision is about seeing, about focusing. It is about allowing the other whether it is a person, a thing, or God to speak to you. Allow the heart to go out to subject, be attentive and open. Only then will you know. Too often we lose contact with people and surroundings, and with God, because we do not give them the attention they require for us to know them. The peasant who spent much time in church was asked by the Curé d'Ars, 'What do you do?' The reply was: 'I look at him and he looks at me.' In the giving of attention heart met heart. We shall see and we shall know.

In knowing we become aware of the mystery of the other, the wonder of each creature or person. The more we know, the more we can be moved and so we move from knowing with the head alone to knowing with the heart. It is then we enter the depths of wonder and awe. We enter into a world of love and praise. If we have failed to do this our journey as well as our work is not complete. Even when we do all of this it is not the end but the 'end which is no end'.

Jim came to church for the next two days but we did not meet up. On the third day he was missing. It was again a wonderful morning and I thought he might have gone for a walk. Later in the day he gave me a call. He wanted me to know that he had gone for a walk before church and the light and darkness around the castle had held him almost in a spell.

> You should have seen it. It was a dark mass in a sea of light. I felt as if I had been like that castle and I wanted to capture it in that mood. I had to rush back and get my camera and a canvas for I knew the mood would not last.

I wondered if he was talking about the castle or himself.

Over the second week Jim was on the island he was painting like he used to. He was totally absorbed in his art. He spent hours trying to capture what was a fleeting moment. When he showed me his work at the end of the week, I felt there was a new light and depth in what he was doing. He had some wonderful photographs of the castle and of the limekilns. He had taken sweeping shots of the shoreline and an odd shot of a few stones or an old post on the beach. Many of the photographs showed a deep interest in light and in shadow.

> This week has helped me to get more than my photographs in focus. More than one thing has touched my heart and captured my attention. I thank you for the time you have given me, we all need people we can talk to and turn to.

Jim's experience reminded me of a story from the Outer Hebrides. A woman was looking after her ill son. Whatever she did for him and whatever treatment he got he did not heal. The illness turned the two of them in on themselves. Illness nearly always turns us in on ourselves. The mother was at her wits' end and the lad seemed to be fading away. This was a time of desolation. Yet in our world the sun is always there and trying to break out. The presence of God does not leave us, even when we feel he is far off or we turn our back on him. The couple came across an injured swan on the shore near their house. The poor bird looked as if it was starving to death. Their hearts went out to it. They took it to their croft and with great difficulty cared for it. Slowly it began to recover; it regained strength and health. At the same time the young lad also began to mend. His healing kept pace with the swan's recovery. The swan had turned their attention away from the illness that beset them and in so doing they moved out of the darkness. By the time the bird flew the lad was well on his way to being fully recovered. In looking after another he had found healing. In moving outside themselves they had turned towards the light.

Another artist, who often visited the island, came to see me because he was depressed. He had a great list of terrible things that had happened to him and his family. I was not surprised that he was depressed. A great shadow had been cast over his life. He was convinced that the world is not a just place and it was often downright awful. He was surprised when I agreed with him on this score. The world can be a very cruel place and a very oppressive place. But I wanted to say the world is not a desolate place. It is a place where we can find light, love and our God: or where love, light and our God seek us. However, the real reason for his coming was he had the problem of taking tablets that dulled his sensitivity. The tablets eased the depression but made him feel unaware of much that was about him. His art and his relationships were suffering. What should he do? As his art and his relationships grew out of his sensitivity there was no easy answer. Too often symptoms are treated and not the cause of the trouble. Often sedatives can be an easy way out. I do believe that there are times when we all need to take medicines and there are many people who do need sedatives to restore a chemical imbalance in the body. As I am not a doctor I could not suggest he gave up taking the pills. I did say he needed to discuss this more openly with his doctor and to see if there was another way of dealing with his present state of mind. We cannot ask God for help if we refuse the help he offers us through the medical profession.

As this man came for help, I tried to do what I could in the short time I was with him. He was a Christian so there were other resources to add to the medicinal ones. How could we find a way for him to walk into the light? I asked him to have a time every day when he would think and thank. Start by remembering you are in the presence of God who loves you. No matter what the world does to you, God loves you. No matter how you feel towards God or about God, he loves you. God is with you. Now think of the day and give thanks for life, for the light, for the world about you. A thankful heart cannot stay for long as a sad heart. In giving thanks for others and to God we learn to appreciate the world and what is about us. This is all I asked him to do but it was a request for him to turn and face the light, with the hope that he could move out of the shadows. Because he was an artist I gave him part of a prayer attributed to St Patrick and asked him to use it as daily affirmation. It begins 'I arise today'. There is a miracle of awakening out of sleep and into a new day. We experience a mini-resurrection, an opportunity for newness of life. The prayer is:

I arise today
Through a mighty strength, the invocation of the Trinity,
Through belief in the threeness,
Through confession of the Oneness
Of the Creator of Creation.

I arise today
Through the strength of Christ . . .
I arise today
Through the strength of heaven:
Light of sun,
Radiance of moon,
Splendour of fire,
Speed of lightning,
Swiftness of wind,
Depth of the sea,
Stability of earth,
Firmness of rock.

I arise today
Through God's strength to pilot me:
God's might to uphold me . . .

(Meyer, 1928, pp. 25–6)

Later that year I received a note from this artist saying, 'The prescription worked – yours and the doctor's.'

Jacob is seen as a strange character in the way he cheats his brother out of his birthright and out of the blessing from his father. This does not mean that God does not love him or cannot work through him. Jacob is sent to find a wife from his kinsfolk in Paddan-aram. On this journey he camps for the night at Bethel. There must have been mixed thoughts as he went to sleep; his father was near to death and his brother was threatening to kill him. In the night he had a vision; he was suddenly aware of the presence of God. Jacob saw a vision of a ladder reaching from earth to heaven with angels ascending and descending upon it. He was aware of God and that he cared for him and went with him wherever he went. When he awoke he said, 'How awesome is this place! This is none other than the house of God, and this is the gate of heaven' (see Genesis 28.10–17). In the darkness of his life and in the darkness of the night shone the love, the light and the presence of God. Desolation turns to consolation.

Francis Thompson was aware for all his troubles:

> The angels keep their ancient places; –
> Turn but a stone, and start a wing!
> 'Tis ye, 'tis your estrangèd faces,
> That miss the many-splendoured thing.
>
> But (when so sad thou canst not sadder)
> Cry; – and upon thy so sore loss
> Shall shine the traffic of Jacob's ladder
> Pitched between heaven and Charing Cross.
>
> (Thompson, p. 133)

For all his troubles Francis Thompson was well aware of heaven in earth and God in man. Now there is a challenge for us all.

Exercises and Reflections

1 Pray

> Lighten our darkness, we beseech thee, O Lord; and by thy great mercy defend us from all perils and dangers of this night, for the love of thy only Son, our Saviour Jesus Christ. Amen.
>
> (Book of Common Prayer)

Or

> Lighten our darkness,
> Lord we pray.

Lighten our darkness
At the end of the day.
Defend us from danger
And perils this night
For the love of Jesus
The Lord who is Light.

Lighten our burden,
Lord we ask.
Lighten our burden
Bring joy to our task.
Give peace in our labour
To work bring your might
For the love of Jesus
The Lord of light.

(Adam, 1992, p. 81)

2 Rest, Read, Ruminate, Reflect, React

Rest   There are times when you have poured out your energy or you feel as if it has been drained from you. This happens to us all. Then you need recharging: you need a power source that will give you new strength. Rest now in the power and peace of God. Know you are in his presence and his power is all about you. Let go and let God. Know we have no power of ourselves; our strength comes from God. Rest your body, let go of all tension and enjoy being with God and in God. Allow his love and his peace to flow into your life.

Open your mind to him and let his presence refresh and restore you. If your mind wanders, quietly say, 'Make me a clean heart O God and renew a right spirit within me.'

The Eclipse of the Heart

Read Ezekiel 37.1–14

Ruminate Walk up and down this valley of dry bones with Ezekiel. It is a place we all know. It is a place of desolation, of despair. Here are the drained of life. You may have said more than once with Israel, 'Our bones are dried up, our hope is lost, we are cut off completely.' This is a place where the heart is eclipsed: it is the land of shadows. No wonder the people of Israel felt like this. In 597 BC King Jehoiachin surrendered Jerusalem to the Babylonian army. Into exile in Babylon went 10,000 of Judah's people. Among them was the young Ezekiel who was only in his twenties. He had been training to be a priest and serve in the temple. In 587 the temple and the city of Jerusalem were destroyed. It is after ten years in captivity and with their precious temple destroyed that Ezekiel seeks to address the people's despair with the promise of consolation. The light has not left them, for God still loves them and is ready to 'resurrect' them. To many this must have sounded totally impossible.

Reflect When we are dispirited we enter the valley of dry bones. We feel wrung out, dried up and unable to achieve anything. Something in us has died for there seems to be no life in us. Let us ask, 'Can these dry bones live?' I have asked this of myself and I have asked it of the Church and of the nation. By ourselves the answer is 'No' but we are not by ourselves. The Spirit of God fills the world and seeks to fill us. God can revive and renew us. The disciples discovered this on the day of Pentecost when suddenly they were all filled with the Holy Spirit. We are not left in the valley and in the shadow of death. We are not alone, for our God waits to come to our aid. That which we see as a breakdown can be the way to newness of life, to a resurrection. It is not something we can make happen but we can prepare for it by keeping our relationship with our God and trusting in him. We need to keep ourselves as open as possible to what is happening around us and to us and to acknowledge that our God is with us.

React   No one is free from entering into the valley of dry bones. Events can quickly bring us to this place. Do you walk in the light of God?

Promise that each day you will put your trust in God, that you will acknowledge his presence, his power and his love. You could slowly affirm this in the words of Psalm 23 if you would like some words to guide you.

3 Pray

> Look, upon us, O Lord,
> and let all the darkness of our souls vanish
> before the beams of your brightness.
> Fill us with holy love,
> and open to us the treasures of your wisdom.
> All our desires are known to you,
> therefore perfect what you have begun
> and what your Spirit has awakened us to ask in prayer.
> We seek your face,
> turn your face to us and show us your glory.
> Then shall our longings be satisfied,
> And our peace shall be perfect.
>
> (Augustine of Hippo, 354–430)

Our Refuge and Strength

One day I suddenly realized that I had within my parish something everyone should have, a refuge box. In fact I had at least two within the parish, one for those on foot and one for travellers in their car. The refuge box is a place of safety where you can go if you have been suddenly caught out and the waves are likely to overwhelm you. Caring people who were concerned about the safety and the lives of others put them there. Let me explain.

For 13 years I was the Vicar of Holy Island, which is a tidal island. The Venerable Bede who was an early authority on tides calls it a demi-isle and says of it and its tides: 'As the tide ebbs and flows, this place is surrounded twice daily by waves of the sea like an island, and twice, when the sands are dry it again becomes attached to the mainland.'

In geographical terms Holy Island is a tombolo, which means it is only an island when the tide is high or rising and the rest of the time it is part of the mainland. This allows tourists to cross the metalled causeway at certain times each day by car. There are times when the sea covers the causeway and the water could totally cover a car. Obviously there are times when you cannot cross and times when you should not attempt to cross. There are plenty of warning notices. Holy Island has more 'Danger' notices than most parishes have on their approach. However like all of life, people do not read or heed notices and so in the summer many cars get themselves trapped in the water. It is always about the same place, so near to the mainland but impossible to travel the last few yards to reach it. No one is suddenly rushed at by the tide. No one is suddenly trapped. If they are in deep water it is their own fault – or at least the driver's. They often blame the water but it is not the sea at fault, the fault is in ourselves. How like much of life. We have made our mistake; now we need help. Getting wet, and possibly frightened, people have to leave their car, which has stalled, and wade through water to the refuge box. This is like a shed on stilts that makes it stand proud of the rising waters. There they are safe from waves or storm.

Because of adventurous living, sin or foolishness we all need a refuge box at times. But it is not a place to live in! It is a shelter from the waves and you can stay there until the storm is past. I have often thought of the refuge box when I have sung

> Jesu, lover of my soul,
> let me to thy bosom fly,
> while the gathering waters roll,
> while the tempest still is high:
> hide me, O my Saviour, hide,
> till the storm of life is past;
> safe into the haven guide,
> O receive my soul at last.
>
> Other refuge have I none;
> hangs my helpless soul on thee;
> leave, ah, leave me not alone,
> still support and comfort me.
>
> (Charles Wesley, 1707–88)

The other thought that has often crossed my mind are the words of Julian of Norwich who lived in times of trouble. She was born in 1342. In 1373 she suffered from what was considered to be a terminal illness, yet lived until about 1417. Hers was the time of the Black Death, the Peasants' Revolt and the battles of Crécy, Poitiers and Agincourt. She saw four kings sit on the throne of England. Julian wrote: 'He did not say, "You shall not be tempest-tossed, you shall not be work-weary, you shall not be discomforted." But he said, "You shall not be overcome." '

There are times in life when we all need a safe haven from the storms, a shelter from the stormy blasts. Anyone who says, 'This is needing a crutch' has never experienced the breaking of a leg or the risk of being overwhelmed. Fishermen have the sense to respect the sea and know when not to venture upon it. I believe that all who are truly alive enter into dangerous and difficult situations and at times need a place of safety and refuge. If you have never needed a refuge you are either perfect or have never risked much. But places of refuge are not meant to be lived in for ever. The refuge box on the causeway is there to rescue you from one tide. Even there in the box is a phone that is a direct line to the emergency services. If the storm of the sea is threatening you too much, or you are being overwhelmed by panic or even if you are soaked and maybe in risk of hypothermia, the phone is for you.

As an aside I would like to tell you what often happens next. You pick up the phone and a voice asks you about yourself and your needs. If you are assessed to be at risk, rescue is set into operation either through the RNLI and a lifeboat or by the RAF and a Sea King helicopter. The Sea King comes and hovers overhead and a man is lowered to you. I have seen this man lowered into a raging sea before in his willingness to come down to where a troubled person was. He comes to where you are. He does not tell you off for being silly nor does he say inane things like, 'It's a beautiful view from here.' He seeks to set you at your ease. Then he explains how you will be fastened to him and gently lifted up, raised up and taken then to a safe place.

You might like to look back at your car as it is being buried by water. It is probably a write-off!

Here is a wonderful image of the incarnation, the resurrection and the ascension. Jesus came down not to reprimand us, nor to admire the scenery but to rescue us from disaster. He came with a purpose: that we may be one with him, that we may be fastened to him and raised with him. He came down not only to be among us but also to lift us up. He descended so that he might ascend. And he takes us with him where storms do not rage. You have been rescued but you might like to look back at what has carried you round; your earthly frame may be a write-off but you will survive.

Places of refuge are necessary in this world but they are meant to give us the power to survive and move on. They are also places where we learn of the love and care of others and that we are not alone in our journey. There are times when we all need to be an escapist.

The young woman looked as if she had not a care in the world. I asked her why she had come to the island and she replied, 'To escape.' I wondered what she was on the run from and if there would be someone in hot pursuit. She was planning to stay on the island as long as she could. She had got a job in one of our small hotels. She repeatedly said when she first met me, 'It is so peaceful here.' I could not help but agree for the island can provide a great deal of peace. But the island is no more peaceful than many other places and in a small community it is often hard to hide anything. The island is often hyperactive with tourists in the season and we are in danger of not having enough time for each other. There are certainly times when we are work-weary and discomforted.

It was not long before I discovered that this escapist had brought all her demons with her. She was the sort of person that demanded attention and if she did not get it she went into

72

depression or threw out insults and innuendoes about the people who did not care enough for her. As a person she could have taken up all your time with her troubles and then complained that you were not giving her enough time. She was a person that needed lots of help and yet sadly soon frightened people away. It was not long before the place where she was working found her too disruptive with the other people who were staying and asked her to leave. I never knew what she was escaping from but I did realize that her demons and troubles followed her. She was on the run but could not escape from herself.

In many ways we are all like this woman; we carry around with us memories, fears, prejudices and a few of our own demons. Some of us carry not only personal memories but also racial hurts and scars that belong to our nation. It just takes someone to press the right trigger and we tend to react as if it was all happening to us again. All seems to be going well when suddenly a shadow crosses our path and we plunge into a darkness that hides the light of the day, coldness sweeps over us and we want no contact with what is around us. Suddenly we can feel dislocated, dispossessed and depressed by what is around us. In 'Bishop Blougram's Apology' Robert Browning describes how suddenly our mood can change for good or for bad:

> Just when we're safest, there's a sunset-touch,
> A fancy from a flower-bell, some one's death,
> A chorus-ending from Euripides,
> And that's enough for fifty hopes and fears
> As old and new at once as nature's self,
> To rap and knock and enter in our soul.

For some, when they feel troubled, the reaction is then to hit out in defence, even though the trouble lies within them. We would usually prefer to blame others than look at our own faults. We would rather change the world around us than to submit to change ourselves. There are people who seem to find no other way of communication than that of constant confrontation. Such people almost need a sign saying, 'UXB, Unexploded Bomb, handle with care'. We all know people that we avoid because they are so explosive and destructive, but do we ever see in them a mirror of our own actions and reactions to the world around us?

There is a cautionary folk tale about a family who were beset by a little demon. This demon caused havoc in the house and with their relationships. In the end they decided there was nothing for it but to move house. They sought to escape their trouble. They packed all their belongings into a cart and set off. They were glad to get away. They had gone only a few miles when a voice from the back of the cart said, 'So, we are moving, are we? Where are we going to now?' They moved but they carried their demon with them! They tried to be rid of the demon but they carried him with them wherever they went.

The Stoic philosopher Seneca writes in one of his letters:

Here is what Socrates said to someone who is making the same complaint: 'How can you wonder that your travels do you no good, when you carry yourself around with you? You are saddled with the very thing that drove you away.' How can novelty of surroundings abroad and becoming acquainted with foreign scenes and cities be any help? All that dashing about turns out to be quite futile. And if you want to know why all this running away cannot help you, the answer is simply this: you are running away in your own company. You have to lay aside the load on your spirit. Until you do that no where will satisfy you.

We are often on the run from ourselves. What we need is not to change our scenery but to allow ourselves to be changed. In Psalm 51 the psalmist cries, 'Create in me a clean heart, O God, and put a new and right spirit within me' (verse 10). He recognizes the need for change within himself. He turns to the Creator, for only the Creator can truly renew us. Renewal and forgiveness are for us part of having all things made new. For this reason I often pray:

> Lord Jesus Christ, you changed water into wine: the
>   common into the precious.
> You healed the troubled mind and brought peace.
> You brought the dead back to life again.
> I ask you for yet another miracle: create a new heart
>   and right spirit within me.

We need to face our inner troubles; at least to know they are there and likely to cause us trouble. Once we know what causes us to react in this way we are on the way to defusing explosive situations. It is good if we are able to share with a loved one or a friend and recognize our troubles for what they are. Though they are history, they are what have made us who we are and they continue to vibrate in our lives.

I was sorry that this young woman would have to leave the island due to her difficulties. In her eyes it would only reinforce how people are not willing to understand or to accept her, she would only feel more rejected and more in need of help and understanding. Sadly she would be passed from group to group as they feared an explosion in their presence. In a parting shot of anger she threatened to bring a case of unfair dismissal against the people that had employed her. Fortunately this did not come to pass and it saved more confrontation and agony.

There is a great deal of darkness and grief in the conscious or subconscious of the modern person. We have to face so much reality in terms of daily news and projected futures. The threat of atomic war is replaced by global warming. We daily hear of wars and strife between nations and are threatened by terrorist actions. Every week we read of food scares and of things that can do us harm. We suffer often from mental overload and at the same time feel incapable of doing much to help in the major situations. We long for help and guidance and do not easily find it. In freeing ourselves from our religious past we have often created a vacuum. As nature abhors a vacuum it is soon filled with something. Very often it is trivial pursuits or our own demons. We were wise to leave behind a god who was only a crutch or only a hiding place. But we have also turned our backs on the God who is our strength and a very present help in trouble. We have lost the God who is the giver of peace, and are no longer at peace with ourselves or with others. To come before the living God is never an escape into a cocooned world but it is a call to live life to the full. Christianity that diminishes a person and their way of life does a dis-service to the Lord who says, 'I came that they may have life, and have it abundantly' (John 10.10). It is a worthwhile exercise to read the Gospels and see how many people found new life and healing through contact with Jesus.

The peace that God offers is not an escape from the storm but the power to live in the storm and the knowledge that in God we will not be overwhelmed. When I am faced with troubles and fear I return to the presence of God. Sometimes I bring to memory the words of Isaiah 43.1–3:

Do not fear, for I have redeemed you;
I have called you by name, you are mine.
When you pass through the waters, I will be with you;

and through the rivers, they shall not overwhelm you;
when you walk through fire you shall not be burned,
and the flame shall not consume you.
For I am the LORD your God,
the Holy One of Israel, your Saviour.

When asked by a young friend if this was 'positive thinking' I
felt I knew what he was getting at and said, 'No. This is reality.
This is where my peace and hope lie. It is not positive thinking
but a living relationship with God and only there in him is my
peace.'

A person who could be an icon – a mirror image – for those
who are on the run is the poet Francis Thompson who was
born in Preston in 1859, the son of a doctor. He studied for the
priesthood and was at Ushaw College, Durham, for seven years.
He left to study medicine but failed to graduate. He then
worked as a shop assistant in Leicester Square, London, and as
a collector of books for a bookseller. He suffered from ill health
and descended into opium addiction. Wilfrid and Alice
Meynell to whom he had sent some of his poems rescued him
from poverty. Francis Thompson died at the early age of 48.
'The Hound of Heaven' expresses his flight from God and
charts well the journey of many an escapist. I have known these
words to fit me well!

I fled Him, down the nights and down the days;
I fled Him down the arches of the years;
I fled Him, down the labyrinthine ways
Of my own mind; and in the midst of tears
I hid from Him, and under running laughter.
Up vistaed hopes I sped;
And shot precipitated,
Adown Titanic glooms of chasmed fears,

From those strong Feet that followed, followed after.
But with unhurrying chase, and unperturbèd pace,
Deliberate speed, majestic instancy,
They beat – and a voice beat
More instant than the Feet –
'All things betray thee, who betrayest Me.'

Later in this poem Francis Thompson hears the voice say:
'Naught shelters thee, who will not shelter Me' and 'Lo! Naught
contents thee, who content'st not Me.' The poem ends with the
lines:

Ah, fondest, blindest, weakest,
I am He Whom thou seekest!
Thou dravest love from thee, who dravest Me.

This poem has much to say to any who are seeking to escape
from God and we would do well to heed its message.

In Psalm 139.7–12, after affirming that God has searched
him out and knows him and all that he does, the psalmist wonders for a moment if there is a way of escape. He asks, 'Where
can I go from your spirit? Or where can I flee from your presence?' There are more people seeking to escape from God than
to escape to him. To turn away from God is to lose the centre of
our life and to become self-centred, to be egocentric. To flee the
presence is to take the road to desolation. But the psalmist discovers we may seek to leave God but God does not leave us.
God can be found in the heights and in the depths of life. Even
our darkness is no darkness with God. When the Psalms talk of
Sheol this is the land of shadows; some would say it is death or
the place without God. Sheol can stand for drink, and drugs,
for immorality or wickedness; God is still there and waiting for
us to turn. The psalmist says there is no place without God.

God is ever with us, and waiting to come to our help. He will be not only our refuge but also strength for us to go out in the power of his Spirit. The lives of so many saints and missionaries have witnessed to this in their proclamation of the presence and power of God. Even when we lose our hold on God, we are still held by his power and in his hand. He will never force himself upon us but we cannot escape from him as long as we live. We can choose to ignore him or to deny him but he is there. God does not die or disappear when we turn our backs on him but we are choosing darkness and not light.

Exercises and Reflections

1 Walk with God into the dark places of your memory and your fears and pray:

> Here is my heart, O God,
> here it is with all its secrets;
> look into my thoughts, O my hope,
> and take away from me all wrong feelings:
> and let my eyes be ever on you
> and release my feet from the snare.
>
> (Augustine of Hippo, *Confessions*, IV.6)

2 Rest, Read, Ruminate, Reflect, React

Rest Know that God accepts you as you are. He comes to you in love. Let God's love surround you. Rest in his presence. Let your body relax and your mind be at peace. If your mind wants to wander say quietly,

> You, Lord, are in my life,
> your presence fills it.
> Your presence is peace.

You can easily change 'life' in the first line for 'heart', 'home' or 'mind'.

Read Luke 8.22–39

Ruminate Try and picture the events. Use each of your senses to do this.

Scene 1 See the storm coming, look at the waves, feel the boat rocking, taste the spray, hear and feel the wind. Seek to be aware of the danger as the little boat is being over-whelmed. Even the fishermen are afraid. Jesus sleeps. How often do we let Jesus sleep in our lives and make no attempt to wake him? Hear the call, 'Master, Master, we are perishing.' Without him we will all perish but we are not without him (see John 3.16). Jesus commands the wind and the waves and there is peace. Jesus brings order out of chaos, calm to the storm – not only to the sea but also to the disciples.

Scene 2 See the disciples on terra firma. It is good to be on safe ground. Are we ever? They have landed in a graveyard. To the superstitious and the nervous this can cause a multi-tude of fears alone. Worse, there is a madman there. Many react as if mental illness were infectious. The peace that Jesus brought to the disciples is disturbed again. See the madman approach. His arms are flailing and there are chains swinging from his wrists. He is completely naked. He rages against Jesus. Here is a man full of demons. Jesus is a picture of peace. He does not run away or hide. He calmly asks the man his name. The poor fellow says he is 'Legion'. He thinks he is an army, or was it an army that got him into this state? This poor man is not allowed with the living and so has made his home with the dead. His life is a mini-hell; no, for him it is hell. As Jesus stands before him we wait to see what can be done for this poor man. We may ask with Macbeth:

> Canst thou not minister to a mind diseased,
> Pluck from the memory a rooted sorrow,
> Raze out the written troubles of the brain,
> And with some sweet oblivious antidote
> Cleanse the stuffed bosom of that perilous stuff
> Which weighs upon the heart?

(*Macbeth*, Act 3 scene 1)

Jesus can and does. Soon the man is at peace. He is clothed and sitting at the feet of Jesus. The man would have liked to stay with Jesus but Jesus sends him home and tells him to declare what God had done for him. In Jesus the words of the Psalm come true: 'He stills the roaring of the waves and the madness of the people' (see Psalm 65.7). Our Lord is the Prince of Peace and he brings peace to his people.

Reflect   Do you allow the peace of Christ to come into your life or are you afraid of him like the people from the Gerasene area (Luke 8.37)? God is not just concerned with our spirit; he is concerned with our whole life, our bodies and minds as well as our spirit. God offers us his presence in our darkness and to be with us in our distress. He will not force himself upon us. We may not call upon him but he waits on our call. Will we let this love and this help lie dormant in our lives? Call him and know he offers you his peace. Invite him into your own personal storms, your fears and where you feel laid bare, and let him clothe you in your right mind and bring you his healing. It is in his power you can venture and not fear.

React When you feel angry, rather than count to ten speak to God!

Promise to invite God each day into the troubled areas of your life and relationships and seek his peace. You may like to say throughout the day as an affirmation – that is to make you more aware of the reality –

> You, Lord, are in my life,
> your presence fills it.
> Your presence is peace.

Remember you can easily change 'life' in the first line to 'heart', 'home' or 'mind'.

3 Pray

> I weave a silence on to my lips
> I weave a silence into my mind
> I weave a silence into my heart.
> I close my ears to distractions
> I close my heart to temptations
> Calm me, O Lord, as you stilled the storm,
> Still me, O Lord, keep me from harm
> Let all the tumult within me cease
> Enfold me, Lord, in your peace.

(Adam, 1985, p. 7)

Who is in Control?

We were lucky to have Ernest as a churchwarden. He was Ernest by name and earnest by nature. He was what you could call a self-made man. Through self-discipline and hard work he had achieved much. He had a high executive position in a large company. He was a good organizer and made sure things were done properly. The church gained much from his generosity and time. Every year he opened his house and garden to the parish for a garden party and a meal. The proceeds of the day were divided between the church and a relief organization. I suspected that Ernest never let the amount be below a certain figure. If it was a smaller turnout than usual he obviously topped the money up. You would think we were blessed with such a man, and in many ways we were, but Ernest had a dark side for Ernest was a control freak.

When we had a business meeting everything had to centre on Ernest; what he thought and what he was doing. He easily managed to browbeat the gentler souls. He brandished his diary like a weapon. When we tried to fix dates he demanded that all was fitted in around his tight schedule. There was no doubt that he did have a very full diary. Sometimes, when we had put ourselves out to fit in, at the last minute he told us he could not come, 'Something of consequence had turned up'. An image from *The Little Prince* by Antoine de Saint-Exupéry used to flit across my mind. A businessman occupied the fourth planet the little prince visited. This man was so busy he did not even raise his head when the little prince arrived. The little prince tried to talk to him but the man was too busy counting and had got to five-hundred-and-one million. He spent his life counting and recounting the stars. He did not let anyone disturb him because he said, 'I am concerned with matters of consequence.' The little prince then left the man alone.

If we decided on doing something without Ernest he wanted to know why he was not consulted; Did we not know the expertise he had in this area? We were regularly reminded how able he was and how willing he was. Ernest's favourite word was 'I': 'I can help. I have the talents. I can give. I can support that. I am busy. I have a job, you know.' I did not doubt any of it but I was tired of hearing Ernest promoting himself.

Due to the efforts of Ernest as churchwarden, the church was still using the 1662 Prayer Book and the King James Version of the Bible. I admire and use both of these but we need to see that we do need other forms of worship for many people. Ernest reminded me often of a little jingle that went:

> Our family have been churchwardens
> For a thousand years or so
> And to every new proposal
> We have always answered No!

The crunch came from Ernest when he was made redundant. The firm he worked for went over to computers and needed to lose a third of their employees. This was at every level of the business. Ernest was told he was no longer needed. He was given a wonderful amount of money but that in no way compensated for being told he was not needed. Ernest felt his world had fallen apart. To think that the firm chose to keep a young man instead of him – they needed their brains examining. He really did not think that the company could survive without him.

We all need to learn from the Copernican theory of the world and the sun. For many generations people believed that everything revolved around our little world. It was thought that the earth was the centre of the universe. At the same time we decided that everything was in subjection to man, and that included woman. Copernicus, who was born in Torun, Poland, and studied mathematics and optics at Krakow, published his theory of a heliocentric system where the sun is the centre of the solar system with the earth and the planets moving around it. When this was published in 1543 it received a hostile reception not only from those in science who refused to look in this new way but also from the Church. There was a feeling that God was being challenged by saying we are not the centre of the universe. There are still Christians and churches that see themselves as the centre of the universe and feel that all should rotate around them and what they are doing.

There is a group that I used to talk to that I feared visiting in some ways. They would say to me, 'We were praying and God told us this is what he wants you to do.' They often had very clear instructions and expected me to follow them. What scared me were two things: they knew God's will for me and it coincided with what they wanted from me! I have always found difficulty in deciding what is God's will for me at any given moment. I can look back and see God at work but in the present moment it is often difficult to discern what God requires of me. I know he wants me to love, to live in harmony and to be just and fair in my dealings. I know many things that I should not do. But all of that does not say what God requires of me at a given moment. This has concerned me for a long time. I can remember approaching a member of the community where I was trained, whose motto is 'To the glory of God in doing his will'. His reply was that 'The giddy joke is we often do not know what the will of God is'.

The danger for church or individual is to decide what they like or dislike and impose that on their dealing with the world. We do not allow what is to make an impact because we censor out what we do not approve of. We object to change if it threatens our comfortable way of life. The danger with some forms of religion is that they can be used as a protection from any real encounter with God. There are some things that are beyond our control and need lives and hearts that can be moved and changed. We are forever meeting with God who makes all things new . . . If we allow tradition or our church ritual to shield us from such an encounter, then we use them as an escape and, worse, as a protection against any real dealings with God. If we can prescribe God's will then there is no need to meet up with him.

There is a great danger that many church groups seek a God who is a puppet and can be used to back up their opinions and desires. This was often seen at its worst during the Spanish Inquisition. There was once a famous court in Spain where, when the sentence was to be pronounced, the 'Yes' to guilty or the 'No' to not guilty was performed by a wooden Christ on a crucifix; due to someone manipulating the head of the Christ it would nod or shake! A pity they could not see how sacrilegious such an act is. It is for us to do God's will and not the other way around. Too often the Church presents a very narrow image of the will of God. God is not a restrictive God but One who wants his people to enjoy the glorious freedom of the children of God.

Those who are disillusioned with what such a narrow religion has to offer, and those who have never been attracted to it, should take courage from the fact that God is not enclosed in a world where we can safely comprehend or predict. God will not fit neatly into a book, not even if that book is the Bible. We are blessed with our Scriptures but we are not the people of the Book; we are the people of the living God. We always belong to the borderlands of experience where new vistas are being opened out to us: where new corners are turned, and where we occasionally find ourselves enveloped in mist. New relationships and new ways of doing things are forever being offered to us and this makes life a great adventure. We are being confronted with the mystery of life and of God each day. But we come to the present distracted and with distorted images. We seek to impose upon it our will and refuse to learn or to be changed. Yet suddenly a shift in the light across the landscape, a piece of music, a chance word from someone or the death of a friend will burst into our safety and bring before us hopes and fears. When we are so preoccupied and set in our ways we can be in the presence of a person and not notice them. In the same way we can miss the song of birds and the sunset or sunrise of each new day. We are not actually aware of what is going on around us because we impose upon the present our own agenda. If we are not aware of the wonders that are about us, and the people who come to us, how can we hope to be aware of the God who will not impose himself upon us? Too often we seek similar experiences and the company of like minds. We seek the known when we are called to the unknown and the mystery of the abiding presence of God. It takes a lot of practice and effort to allow the present to be present in our lives. Once we learn to live in the present we discover the world is ablaze with wonder. Elizabeth Barrett Browning says,

> Earth's crammed with heaven,
> And every common bush afire with God:
> But only he who sees, takes off his shoes;
> The rest sit round it, and pluck blackberries,

And daub their natural faces unaware
More and more, from the first similitude.
(*Aurora Leigh*, 1857, book 7, lines 821–6)

Too often we fail to stop, to turn aside and to wonder. We keep to our agendas and we keep tight control or at least to the pretence we are in control. Churchgoers need forever discern between tradition that is the dead weight of history, and tradition that is a doorway into what is happening to us now. It is an exciting moment when we see tradition and the Scriptures as mirrors on what is happening in our lives and in the world and at the same time offering us new adventures and fullness of living. The Church often presents an image of old soldiers talking of past campaigns and living by old codes when it should rather be a like a crack troop setting out into the unknown to explore new territories and to share together in new adventures.

Ernest was able to find many within the Church who were also unwilling to venture, who preferred what has been and wanted it always to be so. Sadly, for such people, the world moves on. Words change their meanings, people change their habits and new ways of seeing and thinking are discovered. If we do not learn to let go and to move on we will be left behind or seen as something quaint but not quite in touch with today. The Church is meant to be at the frontier and not in the backwaters of what is going on. Some city planners have no respect for the old and that is appalling but it is just as bad to try and keep a city or a village as it has always been. Planners have to use great discernment in balancing the old with the new. They are there to assist in that discernment and though given a great deal of control good planners seek to be open to new ideas as ways of doing things. We need the same discernment in the way we build our Church.

I see myself like Ernest, seeking to control my surroundings and wanting things to go my way. I have a lot of self-discipline but good as it is self-discipline does not make disciples. We can be disciples and committed to our God, only when we say, 'Your will be done.' We have to be open to the new ways God offers to us through the insights of others and through where he is leading us.

St Peter was brought up as a Jew with all the rules and regulations that this imposed upon him. To Peter Israel is God's chosen people and the Gospel is for Jews. To mix with gentiles is to become unclean just as to eat certain foods makes one unclean. We meet Peter when he is staying with Simon, a tanner in the seaport of Joppa. Interesting that Joppa is where Jonah had a tussle with doing God's will and caused no end of chaos until he did. Already there is a shift in Peter's life for no strict Jew would stay with a tanner. Simon's house could render a Jew unclean, with its dead animals, with skins and blood around. As the midday sun arose it was normal to rest in the shade. Peter has taken to the housetop, possibly to catch a fresh sea breeze and to escape the smell of tanning. From there he would see the sails of ships in the port. Peter sleeps and has a dream. In his dream all the things that are happening seem to come together. Peter sees a great sail being lowered from heaven and the sail is full of all kinds of animals. A voice speaks to him saying, 'Get up Peter; kill and eat.'

Peter replies, 'By no means, Lord, for I have never eaten anything that is profane or unclean.'

Then the voice says to Peter, 'What God has made clean, you must not call profane.'

This action happened three times and Peter three times said, 'Never'. It is amazing how often we restrict ourselves by saying, 'Never'. We try to keep all of life within the narrowness of our vision and our perception of what is required. We are all tempted to fence ourselves around. 'Never' is often an expression of prejudice, a judging of the future and determining it will be like the past.

Peter awakens puzzled. What was it all about? Almost straightaway there are three men at the door asking for Peter: a Roman soldier and two slaves. They come with the request that Peter go to the house of the centurion called Cornelius of the Italian Cohort at Caesarea. Peter hears the Spirit saying, 'Go with them without hesitation.' The outcome of this is that Peter baptizes Cornelius and his household; the Church is opened up to the Gentiles. For this action Peter has to face criticism from the narrow faction of Jewish Christians at Jerusalem. The same group would dog every stage of St Paul's outreach and mission. In doing the will of God, Peter helped to bring the gospel to the world at large. (You might like to read Acts 10—11.18.)

Exercises and Reflections

1 Pray

> God's will I would do
> My own will bridle.
> God's due I would give,
> My own due yield;
>
> God's path I would travel,
> My own path refuse;
>
> Christ's death I would ponder,
> My own death remember;
>
> Christ's death I would meditate,
> My love to God make warmer . . .

... The love of Christ I would feel,
my own love know.

(Carmichael, 1976, p. 51)

2 Rest, Read, Ruminate, Reflect, React

Rest Know that you do not need to earn God's love for he loves you always. Rest in that love. Relax in the presence of God. Let go all tension from your body and mind. Know you do not have to do anything except accept and enjoy the love that is being offered to you. See if you can still the wandering of your mind by resting in the heart of God. Know you are there in the heart of God and make room in your heart for God.

Read Luke 18.10–14

Ruminate Jesus told the story of the Pharisee and the tax-collector to warn those who thought they were righteous and held others in contempt. There is always a danger in religion to think you can be in God's good books by building up a credit account of good deeds. There are some people who, in doing this, think that God owes them something. They cannot see that love is freely given. Jesus did not think all Pharisees were like this man but he chose an extreme to show the dangers. Here is a good man, a righteous man, a generous man and a well-disciplined man. He is in the temple praying. What more could you ask for? But look at his prayer.

Sadly we are told he prayed with himself. (Many translations have 'with himself' rather than 'by himself'.) We are able to see how self-centred he is. 'God, I thank you that I am not like other people ... I fast ... I give.' This man was the centre of his prayers and not God. His first word 'God'

93

is almost saying, 'God, look at me, what a good boy I am: you must take notice of me.' He was the subject of all his sentences and God the object. It was as if he was declaring God to be in his debt. It is worth noting how many times the Pharisee uses the word 'I' in verses 11 and 12.

Many would wonder about the tax-collector being in the temple praying. Who did he think he was? He had made himself unclean and unworthy by working for the Roman army. He is lucky no one kicked him out! This man did not dare look up to heaven (and rightly so, thought some of the hearers). He could only beat his breast and say, 'God be merciful to me a sinner.' God in his grace and goodness is in control. God is the active member in the request. God is the subject of the sentence and the man sees himself as the object – but that is the object of God's love and mercy. Jesus, as a good story teller, kept the punch line until the end: 'I tell you, this man went down to his home justified rather than the other; for all who exalt themselves will be humbled, but all who humble themselves will be exalted' (Luke 18.14).

Reflect The Pharisee in his self-righteousness found it easy to compare himself with a no-good sort of person in his eyes. He needed to exalt himself at the expense of others. Why did the Pharisee feel so insecure before God that he had to list his own good points? Living by the law and under the law is not the way to freedom or to knowing the love of God. If salvation or forgiveness or love is dependent on us keeping all the rules then surely we are all condemned. We need to come to our prayers aware of the love and the mercy of God. God wants us to come to him as we are. As soon as we turn to him, he is there to welcome us. Too often we see God as a judge ready to pronounce sentence, when we should see him as a loving parent. We cannot please him by rule-keeping

94

unless we are doing this out of love. Above all God wants our love; he wants us to give ourselves to him.

React   Are you still trying to earn the love that is freely offered? God accepts you as you are. Promise that each day you will come before him and rest in his loving presence. Know that in seeking to do his will it is more out of love than out of obedience. If you cannot do it for the love of God you should question why you are doing it at all.

You might like to use each day for a while these words from a hymn:

> Take my life and let it be
> consecrated, Lord, to thee;
> take my moments and my days,
> let them flow in ceaseless praise . . .
>
> Take my will and make it thine:
> it shall be no longer mine;
> take my heart: it is thine own;
> it shall be thy royal throne.
>
> Take my love; my Lord, I pour
> at thy feet its treasure store;
> take myself, and I will be
> ever, only, all for thee.

(Frances R. Havergal, 1836–79)

3 Pray

> Grant to me, O Lord, to know what is worth knowing,
> to love what is worth loving,
> to praise what delights you most,

to value what is precious to you,
and to reject whatever is evil in your eyes.
Give me true discernment,
so that I may judge rightly between things that differ.
Above all, may I search out and do what is pleasing to
    you;
through Jesus Christ my Lord. Amen.

(Thomas à Kempis, 1380–1471)

You Fill Up My Senses

George was a great character. I use to think he ought to have been a gamekeeper on some estate. Instead he lived in a small house and made his living from odd-jobbing. One of the problems with being an odd-jobber is that you are your own boss and that takes a great deal of discipline. Neither George nor his wife was worried about making money or having holidays away from home. In many ways they appeared a picture of contentment. They were happy with a few hens, a nice little garden and their dogs. George had a great knowledge and deep love of country matters. He could show you the nest of a heron or the sett of a badger and delight in just being there.

But behind this cosy reality fell the shadow. George was a heavy drinker. If you want to know how serious this was let me tell you about one of his visits to the doctor. George had not been drinking that morning, or so he said, because he was to be seen by the doctor, who wanted to do various examinations. When George was examined at about 10.00 a.m. he was still more than twice over the legal limit for driving with alcohol in his system! Fortunately George had stopped driving years ago.

I was once given the opportunity to talk to George about his drinking and he spoke with some perception. 'If I am without work and have little to do, I suddenly feel empty. I begin to panic and it is not long before I feel I will implode.' Fortunately I remembered about implosion from experiments in the school chemistry lab. We used to take all the air out of a metal can and then saw how easy it was for it to collapse. Nature abhors a vacuum and will rush to fill it with something or to implode it and destroy the emptiness. George felt like this, as if outward pressures would exert themselves upon him and collapse him. During the conversation George said, 'You have to fill a person with something.' I knew how right he was. We all need to be filled with something.

When you look around you can see people seeking to fill their lives. Obesity is becoming common because people are comfort-eating or trying to fill an emptiness that is not meant for food alone. A great deal of society is ever on the move, seeking new experiences, excitement and adventure. In itself that is not a bad thing but so many hardly ever seem to arrive, are forever in transit and unable to be still. Due to modern technology they are able to fill every silence with images, with words or with music. They spend their lives 'filling time' or 'killing time' and little time in enjoying their own being. A lot of time is spent on the mobile phone and yet they find it hard to communicate well with each other. Much of this going around is about people in flight from the emptiness. Jesus understood well the danger of emptiness and told the story of the haunted house:

> When the unclean spirit has gone out of a person, it wanders through waterless regions looking for a resting-place, but not finding any, it says, 'I will return to my house from which I came.' When it comes, it finds it swept and put in order. Then it goes and brings seven other spirits more evil than itself, and they enter and live there; and the last state of that person is worse than the first.
>
> (Luke 11.24–26)

If we do not fill our lives with the things of God other things will soon fill them. Much of the seeking for excitement and adventure is not as much to extend ourselves as to fill the emptiness we experience within.

A young man came to Holy Island on an almost idyllic day. The sun was shining and the sea was a brilliant blue. The seals were singing on the sandbanks and the terns were chattering overhead. There was a castle to explore and some limekilns, there were good walks with the chance of seeing all sorts of wild life. The place is full of history and down at the harbour there is always something of interest. The young man faced me with his headphones just off his ears and his mobile in his hand, 'What a boring place, there's nothing to do!' He put on his headphones and tuned in to his own music and off he went. It is worth noting that in an age when people are given more freedom, when they have more gadgets to enrich and to extend their lives they become prey to boredom. They have been given things but not relationships and they are starved of the presence. At least they often recognize their emptiness by saying, 'I am bored.' The fault lies not in what is outside of them but what they have not discovered within. Augustine knew about this and said:

> Men go abroad to wonder at the height of mountains, at the huge waves of the sea, at the long courses of rivers, at the vast compass of the ocean, at the circular motion of the stars; and they pass by themselves without wondering.
>
> (Augustine, *Confessions*, X.8)

Nothing in our world is dull or boring if we look deep enough or long enough. It is said that ditchwater is boring but put a microscope to it and you will see it teems with life. People that are bored with the world around them soon become bored with themselves. Boredom is eating away at so many people. To say 'I am bored' is to admit to an emptiness; there is a hole in our lives which surroundings or entertainment cannot fill. Boredom fuels the search for more excitement, for more to fill us. It can easily lead to drink or to drugs. Boredom brings with it the danger of violence or vandalism, when we can do harm to ourselves or to others. Yet nothing can truly fill the space that is made for the eternal. We need to recognize that boredom is a cry of the spirit and it can be God calling us to better things.

Many of our young folk are like a beautifully shaped car. There is no doubt there are some lovely looking people about. If you see this car full of the latest gadgets, there is a wrap-around music system, a navigation system (which would be useful if they knew where they were going!). They have a high-powered and well-tuned engine. Often they have a tank filled to the brim. But the vital spark is not there: the battery is flat and the engine will not start. For all the finesse and finery they cannot get going and the more they try the worse it often becomes. They need a power source outside of themselves to charge them up. They need to wait patiently to be recharged and to be given power.

Sadly few churches encourage a waiting upon the Lord. Churches tend to be as hyperactive as the individuals that make them up. Some churches seem to exist for activity – and that can include lots of hymn-singing and words. We are often in danger of filling people's evenings and their spare time, when we should be filling their hearts through waiting upon the Lord. These are not exclusive one of the other but it does seem that we often have the balance wrong. Too often we alleviate the symptoms and do not seek to cure the illness. Hymns and sermons would not cure George of his emptiness; in some cases they could exacerbate it. Only the eternal could truly fill his emptiness. I would be afraid to suggest that George came to church services until he had spent some time learning of the pre-sence and power of God. George needed a guide, a God-filled person, who could accept him as he is and help him to survive the emptiness by sharing in his journey and leading him to an awareness of the God who calls in the depth of his being.

There is a saying: 'The devil finds work for idle hands.' Because of the way we are made we do not easily cope with emptiness. Often I have heard so-called spiritual advisers saying, 'Just empty your mind.' I want to put up danger signals immediately. Who can empty their mind? We cannot erase all that we know and we do not want to. I find that as soon as I get going on emptying my mind I come across sludge and dirt or dragons and demons. As soon as you get rid of one thought another pops up. If you can get rid of all the good you only then find the darker things let loose. We are not much different in this way to our gardens. If you dig a garden over and clear it of everything but do not put anything in then soon weeds return. Weeds grow naturally in us as well as in gardens. Emptiness will be filled by something. The way to defeat weeds is not just to keep weeding but also to fill the garden, or the mind, with good and useful things. Crowd out as much as possible the weeds and help the good to grow. In writing to the Philippians, St Paul advised them: 'Whatever is true, whatever is honourable, whatever is just, whatever is pure, whatever is pleasing, whatever is commendable, if there is any excellence and if there is anything worthy of praise, think about these things' (Philippians 4.8). Paul realized that the way to conquer evil was by taking good into our lives. Paul realized that even taking and doing good is not enough, we need to allow God to enter our lives and hearts.

I have often compared the mind to a video that cannot easily be wiped clean. Everything you have ever seen, everything you have ever done and all that you have ever heard are recorded. Your whole life is recorded even if you do not remember some of it. On this video are good, life-giving experiences and also destructive and impoverishing ones. For much of our life we have a good control over this 'video' but there are also times when it seems to replay events when someone else presses a button, or it seems to go onto random selection and it turns on to all sorts of things. There are times when I have aimed at being still and quiet and I have had the worst thoughts of the week. The mind is hard to control. Yet there are ways that help to improve what is selected and to keep us on the right track.

There will always be a mixture of good and evil, of creative and destructive influences but we can influence the mixture by deliberate choice. Quite often our attitude to what we do now will influence the way we react in the future.

I realized how George mirrored my own life. I may not have filled myself with whisky but keeping busy, having a full calendar, having every moment filled is just the same. Constant music, television non-stop, video games or puzzles at every opportunity can fill us in the same way as whisky, and cover the deep emptiness within. It is good to fill your house with tenants but only if they are good tenants and not destructive to you or your property. In our world evil cannot be fully evicted from our lives; it cannot be fully conquered; even when we drive it away we do not destroy it. Evil will return and seek entry and sometimes with a greater force than our past has known. Mere negative religion can never be enough. 'You shall not' or 'Don't do that' are bound in the end to failure. True we often need the law to weed out evil but rules cannot save us: they cannot keep us free from trouble. Being self-righteous is not the way to life in all its fullness. But even sterilized emptiness will be invaded. The only way for our minds and our hearts to be safe is to keep them occupied. But then you have to ask with what and with whom.

It is not surprising that love is one of the most wonderful ways of filling our lives, for in any true loving we learn of the love of God. Loving is a movement outside ourselves and towards another and through such loving we move towards the great Other who is God. George was blessed with a loving wife who helped him to overcome his emptiness; sadly the Church did not seem to able to take George a stage further. Too often church people were being religious to fill an emptiness and it was all words and ritual when it should have been the living God.

Philip was not like George: he was very much a townsman and a young lad. He had few commitments and enjoyed living. For a while I had a lot of contact with him. He became one of my regular helpers at church and rarely missed a service. Then he caught the fever of Sunday football. In fact football became his new religion. Philip lived for football. He followed his local Premier League team and was convinced they would always be victorious. He spent over £400 on a season ticket plus the cost of another £10 to £15 a week in getting to a match. His room was filled with posters of his favourite players. He collected books and memorabilia of his team and its players. Most of his waking days were filled with something about football. If he was not watching his team play he was at home watching a game on his television. If you went to see him and a match was on he would hardly notice you and you could not get him to do anything when his team was playing at home. An interesting aside is that Philip thought that anything more than loose change in the collection plate was asking too much when his football was costing him many pounds each week. I was sorry that Philip was actually lost to the Church and had gained a new religion in football and its players. The danger for all of us is that we will create false idols if we do not have contact with the living God.

I am always caught with a dilemma when asked about church-going and some of its rivals. There is tension in many a household on a Sunday when a youngster wants to go horse-riding

and the parents want her to go to church. It is not a straightforward decision; God does not say horse-riding is less important
than churchgoing. God is not against us enjoying ourselves. To
say 'No' to the horse-riding or to the football makes it sound as
if God does not like the joy of living and prefers us to be in
church. God wants us to worship him but he also wants us to
enjoy the world he has given to us. There is many a youngster
that learned to love the world through learning to ride. The
only clear message is, you can pray to God and go horse-riding.
You can thank God for the horse and your ability to get upon
it. I would rather a youngster gave thanks to God in the stable
than they came resentfully to church. An important part of their
learning is that God loves them and the world.

We need to have the courage to show that God is there out
in the world and to be met each day. We all need the Church
and the wisdom it can pass on to us. We need the Church to
help us find meaning and purpose to life, to bring us to God.
We need the support of the Church in times of darkness and to
celebrate the wonders of creation. But we must be sure we are
seeking to bring people to God and not just to fill a pew. People
need to be brought to be recharged, empowered and changed
by God. George and Philip mirrored the emptiness in many
things that the Church offers to the deep needs of the world.
They are as God-filled as we are but we often fail to teach it to
them by the way we live or by offering them activities when we
should be teaching them God-filled stillness.

The disciples had lived with Jesus, shared in his power,
performed miracles, were strengthened by his word and their
fellowship. Then suddenly it came to a halt. True they had suffered from the harrowing experience of the crucifixion and were
in danger of being arrested themselves. But they also experienced the resurrection: they had seen with their own eyes that
Jesus had risen. They had walked and talked with the risen

Lord. Yet we find them hesitant and fearful rather than running about with power. They still felt drained and empty and they were waiting upon God to fill them, to renew them and give them power. As Jesus had directed them, they were waiting to be filled with power from on high. They were all together in Jerusalem to celebrate Pentecost, all in one place. Suddenly there was a sound like a rushing wind. The word used for 'wind' can be used for 'spirit' also. The house was filled with the wind: they were filled with the Holy Spirit. Their emptiness had been filled. In the power of the Holy Spirit they would go out and proclaim the gospel to the world. People would believe not because of their words alone but because they were God-filled people (see Acts 2.1–18).

Sometimes when waiting upon God I like to use the words of a great love song, 'Annie's Song', which John Denver wrote for his loved one, Annie. I apply these words to God:

> You fill up my senses, like a night in the forest,
> Like the mountains in spring time, like a walk in the rain,
> Like a storm in the desert, like a sleepy blue ocean.
> You fill up my senses, come fill me again.

Exercises and Reflections

1 Pray

> Fill Thou my life, O Lord my God,
> In every part with praise,
> That my whole being may proclaim
> Thy being and Thy ways.
>
> Not for the lip of praise alone,
> Nor e'en the praising heart
> I ask, but for a life made up
> Of praise in every part:

Praise in the common things of life,
Its goings out and in;
Praise in each duty and each deed,
However small and mean.

Fill every part of me with praise;
Let all my being speak
Of Thee and of Thy love, O Lord,
Poor though I be and weak.

So shall Thou, gracious Lord, from me
Receive the glory due;
And so shall I begin on earth
The song forever new.

So shall no part of day or night
From sacredness be free;
But all my life, in every step,
Be fellowship with Thee.

(Horatius Bonar, 1808–82)

2 Rest, Read, Ruminate, Reflect, React

Rest   Let your body relax. Have a break from activity and
tension. Seek to make sure you are comfortable and relaxed.
Check each part of your body in turn to see that it is not
tense. Start from your feet and move up to your head. Enjoy
being still. Know that God is with you in the stillness. If the
mind wants to be busy, still its wanderings by saying, 'You,
Lord, are here: you are with me.' Or you might like to quietly
repeat the words of John Greenleaf Whittier (1807–92):

Drop thy still dews of quietness,
till all our strivings cease;

take from our souls the strain and stress,
and let our ordered lives confess
the beauty of thy peace.

Breathe through the heats of our desire
thy coolness and thy balm;
let sense be dumb, let flesh retire;
breathe through the earthquake, wind and fire,
O still small voice of calm.

Read   1 Kings 19.1–13

Ruminate   Elijah was a mighty prophet of God, filled with
the power of God. He has just won a victory single-handed
(do not forget God was working in him) against 450 false
prophets that were leading the people astray. He has with-
stood 450 men and now he is on the run from one woman.
How like a man! True she is a queen and Jezebel is known
to be fierce. Elijah is exhausted by his ordeal on Carmel.
He is utterly drained. Having no energy to fight he flees to
the desert. There he desires to die. Yet, in the emptiness he
is visited and refreshed. The angel of God may well have
been a Bedouin showing the hospitality of the desert people.
Elijah's powers are being restored and he goes a long distance
and shelters in a cave. There in silence he hears God say,
'What are you doing here?' It is worth noticing that God is
there; wherever Elijah went, God would be present and could
ask the same question. God wants Elijah to turn to him, to be
aware of him. And there is a great storm, earthquake, wind
and fire. Elijah wraps himself in his cloak and watches this
display of power. After this there is a silence, stillness after the
storm. In the stillness, Elijah hears God, is filled with God
and able to continue his work for God.

Reflect Emptiness is always capable of being God-filled. The desert in our lives, as well as the actual desert, is where God is often found and where God is seeking to speak to us. Because God will not force himself upon us, it needs us to find a space to let him in – or discover in us the space that is made for him alone. Our cries of emptiness and of boredom are cries to be filled with God. Wherever Elijah went, however he felt, he discovered God was there, waiting for him. Elijah needed the stillness and the emptiness to know his need for God and that God was with him. In his meeting with God Elijah was given new power, he was recharged and refreshed. Now Elijah could go out again in the power of God's Spirit.

React Do we wait quietly upon God? Do we recognize the emptiness that is caused by ignoring the presence and power of God? Promise to make room each day for God to come and fill your life. Fix a place and a time to meet with God and to rest in his presence. Without a fixed time and place there is a danger of not meeting God anywhere or at any time. When you have a fixed time and place it is soon possible to meet God everywhere and at any time. Do not let activity crowd out your quiet time with God.

3 Pray

> I weave a silence on to my lips
> I weave a silence into my mind
> I weave a silence into my heart
> I close my ears to distractions
> I close my eyes to attractions
> I close my heart to temptations.

Calm me, O Lord, as you stilled the storm
Still me, O Lord, keep me from harm
Let all the tumult within me cease
Enfold me Lord in your peace.

(Adam, 1985, p. 7)

Black Holes and Pulsars

In our journeying through time and space we use up energy and need to be renewed. We cannot forever pour ourselves out unless we are in some way refuelled. In my meeting with many people in a day there are days when I end up feeling drained. Sometimes I come to people with my resources already too low and I am of little help or comfort to them. At least I try to listen and give them my undivided attention, but even that demands a good deal of energy. We all need to have times of rest and re-creation, to be with people who will help to refresh and restore us. To have a loving home and someone who cares deeply for us is one of the greatest powers, if not the greatest, in restoring our being. To be with some people we are almost immediately enriched whereas with others we are drained of our resources.

When I was reading about the wonderful mysteries of our universe I was fascinated by the descriptions of black holes and pulsars. It would seem there are many black holes in our universe but they go by almost unobserved; they are not visible to us. A black hole will absorb all that comes into it and diminish it. If it were possible to come out from a black hole you would be much smaller than when you went in. I know some people who are like great black holes: they are greedy for experience, for excitement, for new ventures, for learning and for love. But whatever they get they diminish. Whatever you pour in is cut down to what they want and it often has the life squeezed out of it. Black holes are turned in on themselves and all is measured by their standards. There are people in every part of society who are like this.

Fortunately for us, there are also a lot of pulsars within every community. A pulsar is a star that gives out pulses of light and so pierces the darkness. There are people who radiate light and love to those around them. When you are in their presence their light and their brightness touch you. Pulsars are a joy to experience. There are many people who enrich your life by being with them, who help to recharge your tired body, mind and spirit When on a daily round of visiting or meeting people I always tried to end the day with one of these radiant people, with someone who is a joy to be with and so helped to restore what had been poured out elsewhere. With such people it is possible to have our energies and our perspective restored. Obviously for me, this task often fell to my wife Denise, who has been such a power of strength and joy throughout my ministry and my life.

I have a clergyman friend who has a great sense of humour and refuses to be 'too serious about life'. The Revd Peter had a wonderful way of earthing 'high ideas'.

There is enough 'gravitas' in the Church without me adding to it. We need a bit more levity and the ability to laugh. If we cannot laugh at what we are doing then life has become serious indeed. Christians that are miserable about the world or life do our faith and our God a great injustice.

Peter is one of those people who radiates his faith. You see it in his actions and even in his face. He is a joy to be with.

I can remember on one occasion we were talking about the presence of God and at the same time how God transcends our ability to grasp him. Our minds were greatly stretched with talk of the immanence and the transcendence of God. We were trying to find simple images rather than make theological statements. We explored how some nations, such as the Celtic nations, had a great sense of reverence and at the same time an awareness of the ever-abiding presence, a presence that brought light and laughter into their lives. I told Peter of one of my favourite Celtic prayers from the *Carmina Gadelica*, 'The Path of Right', beginning with its introduction:

> When the people of the Isles come out in the morning to their tillage, to their fishing, to their farming, or to any of their various occupations anywhere, they say a short prayer called 'Ceum na Corach', 'The Path of Right', 'The Just or True Way'. If the people feel secure from being overseen or overheard they croon or sing, or intone their morning prayer in a pleasing musical manner. If, however, any person, and especially a stranger, is seen in the way, the people hum the prayer in an inaudible undertone peculiar to themselves, like the soft murmur of the ever-murmuring sea, or like the far-distant eerie sighing of the wind among the trees, or like the muffled cadence of far-away waters, rising and falling upon the fitful autumn wind.
>
> (Carmichael, 1976, pp. 48–9)

The whole idea of this fascinated him and we both agreed that prayer life for so many people had become something attached to church and not to their daily tasks. We need to make God at home in our homes and to let God be at work in our work. God is not concerned only with religion but with all of life. The prayer that follows made Peter laugh out loud and he promised to use it with some gusto the next time he walked down the aisle for a service.

115

My walk this day with God,
My walk this day with Christ,
My walk this day with Spirit,
The Threefold all-kindly:
Ho! Ho! Ho! the Threefold all-kindly.

My shielding this day from ill,
My shielding this day from harm,
Ho! Ho! both my soul and my body,
Be by Father, by Son, by Holy Spirit:
By Father, by Son, by Holy Spirit

Be the Father shielding me,
Be the Son shielding me,
Be the Spirit shielding me,
As Three and as One:
Ho! Ho! Ho! as Three and as One.

(Carmichael, 1976, p. 49)

Peter said it was important to let people know we actually rejoice in and enjoy the company of God, that his presence makes us able to laugh. For too many people God is a God who is far off and does not seem to really touch their lives. We need to walk again with God and know that he walks with us. This reminded me of one of the first times, when I was a young teenager, that I was deeply moved by a song. It was Mario Lanza singing, 'I'll walk with God from this day on'. I was amazed that such a thing was a possibility and even then thought what a wonderful way it would be to live. Later I discovered, in the prayers from the people of the Hebrides, how a group of people were on easy speaking terms with God. I discovered prayers of the workplace and of the home that welcomed God each day into their lives. I often saw them as prayers of the hearth and heart for they started with the rekindling of the house fire in the morning and the re-warming of the heart towards God. As the woman of the house opens up the smouldering peat fire in the morning and often needs to blow it into life she says:

> I will kindle my fire this morning
> In the presence of the holy angels of heaven . . .
> God kindle thou in my heart within
> A flame of love to my neighbour.
>
> (Carmichael, 1983, p. 231)

Very often on a cold winter's morning Peter and I have been in church when it is very dark. Before putting on the electric lights we have sat in the darkness with the other worshippers – such a darkness is a symbol of our lives without God. Then someone lights a candle and welcomes the day and the light as gifts of God. Then from *Common Worship* we say: 'The night has passed, the day lies open before us; let us pray with one heart and mind.' A silence is kept.

> As we rejoice in the gift of this new day;
> So may the light of your presence, O God,
> Set our hearts on fire with love for you;
> Now and for ever. Amen.
>
> (*Common Worship*, 2005)

I like to think that this is a meaningful remnant of the old heart and hearth prayers when we ask God who gives us light to set our hearts on fire for love of him. In the dark days of winter or whenever we experience a 'dark day' this is a good action to put us in touch with the Lord, the giver of light. It is an action that says the God who transcends all our ideas and thoughts about him is present and with us this day. The God our mind cannot grasp is there and held in our hearts.

117

Peter often expressed his fears about those who brought God down to their own level and forgot his 'otherness'. He wanted us to always proclaim the God who is greater than all our thoughts or dreams: God who is above all that we can ever say about him. But at the same time a God with whom we have to do, a God in our midst. God is not separated from us by distance. God is ever near. It is not a spatial separation but one of his 'otherness' or what the Scriptures call 'holiness'. The wonderful thing is that we can share in that holiness. Peter believed that people who were deprived of the otherness in life had allowed something in them to die and allowed all of life to become like a game of *Trivial Pursuit*.

Peter introduced me to a book called *A Rumour of Angels* and especially drew my attention to a statement towards the end of the book:

A rediscovery of the supernatural will be, above all, a regaining of openness in our perception of reality. It will not only be, as theologians influenced by existentialism have greatly over emphasized, an overcoming of tragedy. Perhaps more importantly it will be an overcoming of triviality. In openness to the signals of the transcendence the true proportions of our experience are rediscovered. This is the comic relief of redemption; it makes it possible for us to laugh and play with a new fullness.

(Berger, 1970, p. 119)

We need to recapture a reverence for our world, for each other and for God.

In his book *The Go-Between God*, John Taylor says, 'There is nothing more needed by humanity today . . . than the recovery of a sense of "beyondness" in the whole of life to revive the springs of wonder and adoration.'

Peter loved to tell stories, and to earth much of our talk about transcendence he told me this lovely tale.

The pope invited a rabbi to the Vatican. Obviously the rabbi saw this as an honour and the chance of a wonderful experience. While in the pope's own apartments the rabbi noticed a gold telephone and asked what it was for. 'That is my direct line to God,' said the pope.

'Can I use it?'

'Of course you can,' said the pope.

The rabbi made his call and then asked the pope how much it cost.

'To you 10,000 lira and cheap at the price,' said the pope.

Later the pope paid a return visit to the rabbi and discovered there a similar phone. 'Is that what I think it is?' asked the pope.

'Of course,' replied the rabbi. 'We have always had a direct line to God.'

After the call the pope asked how much such a call cost.

The rabbi replied, 'To you nothing. It is just a local call.'

Peter always laughed heartily at his jokes and then proceeded to ask if you had got the point, 'Not only is it a local call but it is the only line you can get when even your batteries are flat!' How I enjoyed the brightness of a fellow priest and believer who is full of the joy of living and of knowing the love of God. Peter is a true emitter of light, a pulsar. Peter took to heart the words of Jesus when he said, 'Let your light shine before others, so that they may see your good works and give glory to your Father in heaven' (Matthew 5.16).

When I was in my teens I used to act as a server at Holy Communion on weekdays. Often in the early morning there was only the celebrant there and myself. But we were surrounded by angels for they were painted on the reredos and all in gold they stood on posts at each corner of the altar. There we stood in silence for a few minutes to prepare ourselves for approaching the mystery of God. Then we said Psalm 43 from the Book of Common Prayer antiphonally. I felt I had the best verses, getting the even verses. We both knew the psalm off by heart. I mean heart for it was in worship we learnt it rather than in study. One of my verses said: 'That I may go unto the altar of God, even unto the God of my joy and gladness' (Psalm 43.4, BCP). Another said: 'O put thy trust in God: for I will yet give him thanks, which is the help of my countenance, and my God' (Psalm 43.6, BCP).

Not only is God a God of joy and gladness, God is good for beauty treatment! If you want a facelift, if you want to look radiant come to God with thanksgiving. There are so many people with furrowed brows, downcast faces and sad eyes. They are lacklustre people; there is no shine to them. You can see in them that wealth, activity and travel are not enough. Our appetites will never be satisfied until we are filled with God and his love. Once we are filled with his light, it can be seen in our eyes, our faces and our actions.

There is a lovely story about Moses in Exodus 34.29–35 that tells us when Moses had been talking with God his face shone. Whatever you make of the way the story is told, there is no doubt that Moses was radiant with the light and love of God.

Does your life mirror the love and the light of God? Remember you are made in his image.

Exercises and Reflections

1 Pray

> God be in my head, and in my understanding;
> God be in my eyes, and in my looking;

God be in my mouth, and in my speaking;
God be in my heart, and in my thinking;
God be at my end, and at my departing.

(*Pynson's Horae*, 1514)

2 Rest, Read, Ruminate, Reflect, React

Rest   in the presence of God. Let his love, his light and his peace flow into your life. You need make no effort, only to know you are in the heart of God. If your mind wants to wander bring it back by saying, 'God is here. God loves me. God gives me his light.' In time you should be able to bring it back by lovingly saying 'God' and resting in his love. Make sure that your whole body is relaxed and able to rest in his light and peace.

Read   Luke 14.15–24. This story is meant to sound a little absurd!

Ruminate   Get yourself into the story. Imagine you are poor and not quite sure where your next meal will come from. Someone with great riches invites you to a banquet! He wants you to be filled, to be satisfied. He wants to make sure there is no gnawing emptiness inside you. In our times this is an invitation we would put up somewhere to be seen. You are asked to be with a very generous person. The date and the time are fixed, you are told well in advance. Then you are sent a reminder, 'Today you are invited to the feast.' If you ignore this invitation you will be poorer – and hungry. Ignore this and you will regret it. But the excuses come pouring in:

'Sorry, I am busy. I have bought a field and will be occupied looking at it.'

'Sorry, I cannot come. I have bought some oxen and must go and test them out.'

'Sorry, I have other things on my mind. I have married a wife and cannot come.'

You must see the absurd side of these excuses. Would you buy a field without looking at it – or a house? If you have bought it, it will not go away. You could look at it after seeing the king. Would you buy five yoke of oxen, or a car without a test drive? If you have bought it the deed is done. Trying them out could wait.

With the last excuse you must remember this is a story from the East. Do you think he would let his wife stop him? She does not prevent him but he wants to blame her. He cannot be bothered to make space for the banquet, so he blames someone else for his excusing himself. How often do we blame the pressure of others for not coming to the banquet of our God?

Reflect They that excuse themselves exclude themselves. The invitation is there but we choose to ignore it. We are offered all the riches of the love of God and we choose to occupy ourselves with other things. We are offered the light of God and we choose to walk in darkness. God actually invites us to come to him and we declare we are too busy. We are preoccupied. There is a law of nature, a law built into out world, that says, 'No two things can occupy the same space at the same time.' We are in danger of filling our lives with anything but our God. This filling of ours will never satisfy us, there will be an inner hunger and yet we excuse ourselves. Hard to believe, is it not? Yet we know it is true. God does not exclude us from his presence but those who excuse themselves exclude themselves. Perhaps like many in Bethlehem you display a sign which says, 'No room at the inn'!

React Promise to make room in your life for God. Accept his invitation to come into his presence. Write it into your diary. Make space each day to rejoice in the presence and to relax into the light, the love and peace of God.

3 Pray

> O Lord my God,
> teach my heart where and how to seek you,
> where and how to find you.
> Lord, if you are not here but absent,
> where shall I seek you?
> But you are everywhere, so you must be here,
> why then do I not seek you? . . .
> Lord, I am not trying to make my way to your height,
> for my understanding is in no way equal to that,
> but I do desire to understand a little of your truth
> which my heart already believes and loves.
> I do not seek to understand so that I may believe,
> but believe so that I may understand;
> and what is more,
> I believe that unless I do believe I shall not understand.
>
> (Anselm, 1033–1109)

The Image of God

In the very first chapter of Genesis we are told, 'God said, "Let us make humankind in our image, according to our likeness . . ." So God created humankind in his image, in the image of God he created them; male and female he created them' (Genesis 1.26–27). Not only are we fearfully and wonderfully made, we are made to reflect our Creator, to be the icon of God. An image is a representation of a person in the way that a painting or a mirror represents that person. People should be able to look at us and see something of God; we should reflect his qualities of love, of the ability to create, to make and to mend. If a representation does its work well it then becomes a manifestation. The perfect icon or image is Jesus Christ. To see what God is like we can look at Jesus. Jesus reveals God to us in ways that we can grasp, that we can see and understand.

Eikonion is the diminutive form of *eikon*, which is used of a portrait in words of the person. This was as near as the ancient world could get to a photograph. When a legal document was signed, a bill of sale or an IOU, the contracting parties would be described. This was not just a sketch but a revelation of the person. To be God's image means to reveal him and also to share in his properties. A fisherman friend of mine was always 'making and mending'; how like God! Irenaeus said: 'The glory of God is a living man: and the life of man is a vision of God.' The human fully alive, responding to the reality of God, to the world, to others and to his or her own being reveals the glory, the very presence of God.

Sadly we belong to a fallen world where the image has been marred, disfigured, and often covered over. The image has been impaired; it is out of focus, but it has not been destroyed. Beneath all the layers of sin, of living below par, of missing the mark there are still vestiges of the divine image no matter how distorted they might be. Every one of us is made in God's image, and the potential for revealing him, sometimes even unknown to ourselves, is still there. It may take some time for us to begin to reflect the glory of God, to show his presence in and through our lives, but it is for this we are made.

To look at it from a different angle it is worth considering the teaching of a rabbi. The rabbi set a question for his pupils:

'After finishing the first five days of creation the Scriptures say, "God saw that it was good." On the sixth day when he created the human God is not reported to have made the same remark. What conclusion can you draw from that?'

A pupil was quick to reply, 'We can see that the human is not good.'

'I would not think that is correct,' said the rabbi. 'Surely all that God creates is good.'

He then explained to his pupils that the Hebrew word for 'good' in Genesis is the word *tov*, and is better translated as 'complete'. God did not declare the human as complete for the human is created incomplete and we must work with our Creator to reach our potential. We must make efforts to be God's icon, and to become more and more in his image. For the Christian the true image of God, the way we see God most clearly is in Jesus Christ. When Jesus dies on the cross, St John tells us his last words were, 'It is finished.' These are not words of defeat but of triumph. They mean, 'It is completed.' In Jesus we see the image perfectly. We see in the man Jesus the One who does the Father's will and reveals his glory.

In the second story of creation 'The LORD God said, "It is not good that the man should be alone; I will make him a helper as a partner" ' (Genesis 2.18). The human is made to reflect God's image through relationships, through love, through sharing with others. The human alone is incomplete and could not well reflect the image of God. If we believe in the Three Person God, we are saying that persons in relationship are the very fabric of our world. If we are to be God's image we are to do so in relationship to others. The human is not meant to be alone and our personality suffers if we are left alone. Solitary confinement for any length of time is one of the worst punishments or acts against another we can commit. To refuse to communicate or to be loving will also distort the image we are meant to portray. On the other hand to see a young couple adoring each other and their child, holding each other in love and affection, is to see something close to the true image of God.

There are times when we feel far removed from God and his image. It is important to remember that feelings are often liars. God is ever near and we can reflect his glory in our lives. There are times when I have been studying and the words have become dead and dry, times when my prayers have been a struggle. Often these are times when some relationship is also a struggle or disturbed. It is then I come back to a little verse I learned a long time ago, from where I do not know:

> I sought my God, my God I could not see.
> I sought my soul, my soul eluded me.
> I sought my brother/sister and I found all three.

There is no doubt we are God's image in relationship. As Christ is the complete image of God on earth, the joy of any Christian is to see Christ in others and to be Christ to others. Go to God in your prayers with people in your heart. When you approach him bring someone in your heart to him. Then through prayer and meditation when you meet anyone know that God is in you, is in your heart. Reflect upon this and become more and more a clear image of God.

Select Bibliography

Adam, D., 1985, *The Edge of Glory*, Triangle.

Adam, D., 1989, *Tides and Seasons*, Triangle.

Adam, D., 1992, *Power Lines*, Triangle.

Berger, P., 1970, *A Rumour of Angels*, Penguin.

Carmichael, A., 1963, *Carmina Gadelica*, Vol. 1, Scottish University Press.

Carmichael, A., 1976, *Carmina Gadelica*, Vol. 3, Scottish University Press.

The Cloud of Unknowing, 1961, trans. Clifton Wolters, Penguin Classics.

Gardner, W. H. (ed.), *Gerard Manley Hopkins*, 1953, Penguin.

Hansen, T., 1991, *Seven for a Secret: Healing the Wounds of Sexual Abuse in Childhood*, Triangle.

Julian of Norwich, 1980, *Enfolded in Love*, trans. members of the Julian Shrine, ed. R. Llewelyn, Darton, Longman & Todd.

Lewin, A., 2004, *Watching for the Kingfisher*, Inspire, Methodist Publishing House.

Meyer, K., 1928, *Irish Poetry*, Constable.

Osborne, J., 1957, *Look Back in Anger*, Faber & Faber.

Principles, 1930, SSM Press, Kelham.

Rowling, J. K., 1997, *Harry Potter and the Philosopher's Stone*, Bloomsbury.

Saint-Exupéry, A. de, 1962, *The Little Prince*, Penguin.

Selections of Ancient Irish Poetry, 1928, trans. Kuno Meyer, Constable.

Sillitoe, A., 1960, *The Loneliness of the Long Distance Runner*, W. H. Allen.

Select Bibliography

The SPCK Book of Christian Prayer, 1995, SPCK.
Teilhard de Chardin, P., 1975, *Le Milieu Divin*, Fontana.
Thompson, F., *Selected Poems of Francis Thompson*, Methuen.